# Real Estate Magic

# What You Ought to Know About the Resurgence of Real Estate Investing

## By Don Loyd

***Real Estate Magic***
*What You Ought to Know About the Resurgence*
*of Real Estate Investing*

DreamMaker Press, LLC
Denver, Colorado

SBN-13:
978-1463733421

ISBN-10:
1463733429

First Printing

## TABLE OF CONTENTS

## The Beginning

Stop thinking a paycheck will secure your dreams— it won't. The focus of most people is money—as in a job— trading time for money. This kind of thinking, although embraced by the masses and accepted as conventional wisdom, is a severely limiting mindset.

The problem with trading time for money is you are limited by the number of hours in a day. In order to experience true financial freedom you must change the way you think about money, and money in relationship to time. Start thinking about how money can be working for you.

Real estate investing is the single most powerful avenue for creating wealth. It's a natural fit for women or men. Yet few have entered into this field. Why? I think mainly that is because women simply are not aware of the powerful potential real estate investing holds for them. The truth is, with a small investment of time almost anyone can open the door to the dreams they hold most dear: college education for the kids, a secure retirement, and time to savor life.

Get ready for a great ride.

Don Loyd

## Why Invest in Real Estate?

### Introduction

It has occurred to me that too few are involved in real estate investing. Why is that? It likely goes back generations, like many of the antiquated customs of our forefathers.

One theory is that real estate investing requires commitment, education, and risk. Those three things *of which you are capable*, but are all things that you have little time for after your day job, your dad/mother job, your husband/wife job, and your social functions. After all, there are only 24 hours in a day.

Suppose you could obtain an education that cuts the time needed to pursue those opportunities to the bare minimum and suppose you had a resource to simplify the steps. If so, you could spend your valuable minutes earning valuable dollars, instead of learning tough lessons through trial and error. This book is that education and resource.

Here's the truth: All of us can feel a loss of control or vulnerable when they are unable to provide our children with basic needs. It's difficult to maintain a positive, productive attitude when you are constantly living on the edge of survival. Your present-day reality does not have to continue. You can break the cycle of poverty or dependency and begin to live with positive expectancy and confidence.

Maybe your interest is not financial and you are not included in the group just mentioned. It could be that you have a very successful career and have had a lucrative life with all the perks, and the only thing you really desire is time. The demands of your job have been keeping you on a treadmill where you are busy and productive, but you're not really happy and you want something more in life. You want to know that you can succeed on your own. You want to spread your wings.

Money is simply a vehicle for which we can trade our time, knowledge, and services for goods that meet our needs and desires. The more specialized you become, either in knowledge or skill, the more demand there will be from people who will pay you for your time, abilities, and services. The supply and demand theories that you learned in high school economics still hold true today.

When I was a 14 years old, I worked in the fields cutting grapes and picking plums. In exchange for my labor, I was paid a few cents per box. When I was 15 years old, I was hired as a stock boy at J.C. Penney. I traded 1 hour of my time for $1.25. As my experience, knowledge, and expertise grew, so too did my payment per hour.

I worked at construction in my early 20s and earned more than $10 an hour. That was a great wage for the time and enabled me to buy new houses and cars and spend extended weekends in San Francisco, California. The reality was I was putting in long hours of back-breaking work for my weekly paycheck. The job resulted in a back injury and chronic back pain that has limited my physical activity.

The problem with trading time for money is you are limited by the number of hours in a day. To experience true financial freedom, you must change the way you think about money and money in relationship to time. Instead of looking for a job that will pay you a specific hourly wage, start thinking about money in a different light.

Suppose you could provide a service that is not measurable by dollars earned per hour and that fulfills a need that will benefit others. For example, I work with people who think they can't afford to buy a home. I show them how to rebuild their credit, pay only a little money down, secure a great house, and enjoy a reasonable profit later on. The best part is while I am helping this person, I am also earning a significant income. The scenario is a true win-win situation, perhaps unlike your current scenario where you are underpaid for your time and your employer is gaining as a result.

I also work with people who want to earn a living in real estate investing. By sharing my experience, knowledge, and past successes, I have shattered my old reality (sweating for dollars per hour) and replaced it with a winning proposition for all involved, making everyone dollars along the way. I have learned to work smarter, not harder, and I am going to share that education with you now.

### The Road to Financial Security is Starting Your Own Real Estate Investment Business

As long as a demand exists for your knowledge and skills, you will always have a source of income if you know how and when to use them. More millionaires are made through real estate than any other single business.

You can be one of those if you believe you can and you educate yourself about the process. The great thing about being a real estate investor is that you can accomplish many of your goals without having a large nest egg or start-up funds. No other investment allows for appreciation and positive cash flow as easily as real estate.

You can literally go from broke to a positive monthly cash flow and a million dollars in net assets in less than a year if you work smart. This is not some "get rich quick" scheme, and I hesitate mentioning the million-dollar potential because I do not want this education associated with any late night commercials. This is about giving you knowledge that will help you become successful.

To further legitimize the education you are about to receive, I'll even bring Uncle Sam into it. The government encourages you to get into the real estate investing business. They offer many special tax considerations that equate to more money in your bank account. They offer special financing for various needs. They help people on limited incomes pay their rent. And, if you choose, you can even defer paying your taxes until you retire. The government has set up a host of opportunities that make real estate investing very attractive. And all you need do is learn the process.

I will point you in the right direction, as well as cut through the clutter and all you do NOT need to know. I will show you how to break free to live a satisfying, secure, full life where you can put your own goals before those of your employer. You do not need a degree, you do not need special tools, you don't have to run to the bank and get a business loan, and most importantly, you do not have to be a man.

The opportunities in the real estate industry are not covered with the glass ceiling that still exists in the business world and that women almost always eventually reach. The possibilities in real estate investing are limitless. There is no one to tell you that you can't earn more money or tell you that you cannot be as successful as everyone else who has succeeded before you.

Can you do it? The answer to that question depends on how you think. If you think you can, you're right. If you think you can't, you're also right. It is your choice. Consider this book your first lesson in real estate investing. It gives you the information and encouragement to change your life, but the end result will be up to you.

You don't need any special gifts or talents. If you can follow a recipe, you can also be a successful real estate investor because the recipe, which I will give you, is just as simple.

**True Life Story**

When I was in the second grade, I came up with a plan to set up a roadside stand and sell apples I collected from nearby orchards. I enlisted my brother's help and together we set to work with dollar signs dancing in our heads. Unfortunately, we didn't sell any apples that day and if I remember correctly, we ended up taking the apples to our mother who made applesauce from our supply. The fact that I failed didn't seem to bother me. I kept thinking and planning. In a comic book I found a coupon advertising a business opportunity, mailed it in.

I started my very own door-to-door greeting card sales company. As you might imagine, it wasn't much of a company, but nevertheless, I knocked on the doors of our neighbors and talked to friends and sold boxes of greeting cards. My mother was my best customer.

With those experiences, I began to see the advantage of repeat customers and started a TV Guide® sales route that ran on Saturdays. I would receive my weekly allotment of TV Guides and hit the sales route. When I was 12 years old, I hit the big time. I had a paper route that paid big bucks—a penny for each paper delivered.

I seemed destined to a life of marketing and sales, which is quite interesting once you find out what I had to overcome to achieve that life. From early childhood, I had a speech impediment. I stuttered. Understanding what I was saying was almost impossible at times. My "disability" was bad. I entered speech therapy in the first grade, and although I continued for many years, it didn't seem to help. Finally, when I was a freshman in high school, I completely discontinued speech therapy.

I was often the brunt of jokes, called names, and made fun of by my peers. In high school, I might be walking down a hall and someone would say, "Stutterin' Don, how's it going?" Adults tolerated me and often tried to finish my sentences when I couldn't get the words out, much to my frustration and annoyance.

In 1967, I tried to enlist in the Army but was rejected because my speech impediment was too severe. This was during the height of the Vietnam War, and they were taking almost every young man with a beating heart.

Soon after my Army rejection, I married my wife, Becky, and we had a large church wedding. I didn't want to repeat my vows because I didn't want everyone hearing me make a mess of things. However, since the vows are the central part of a wedding ceremony, I couldn't avoid saying them. When it was my turn to repeat our vows, I just mumbled some sounds so the preacher could hear something.

As hard as my speech impediment was to endure, I was determined not to let it stand in the way of my dreams. I decided that I was in charge of my own life, not those who poked fun or ridiculed me. My success, if any, was up to me.

I contacted a friend of a friend who had a company selling fire alarms door-to-door. My friend told me about all the money he was making. I knew he drove a new Cadillac El Dorado, wore great clothes, had a nice house, and owned a lot of real estate. I wrote him a letter expressing my desire to go to work for him, rather than call, because I didn't want him to know about my speech impediment. He later told me he already knew about my speech impediment and hired me because of it. He said the fact that I wanted to succeed overrode any handicap I had. I believed him, took some sales training (principles I still use today), and started knocking on doors.

Picture the scene: an awkward-looking, 130-pound kid who could barely communicate knocking on doors and trying to get the person inside to purchase an expensive product. Looking back, I must have been laughable. Today it's very difficult to tell that I ever had a speech problem. I cannot put my finger on any one thing that was the genesis of my transformation but today I speak frequently and persuasively to all sizes of groups. I own several companies that enjoy incomes in the millions of dollars. I lead a very successful real estate investment club and ran for a seat on our local County Commission as well as the State Senate.

The story is not that I had a speech problem. The story is "So what! I *had* a speech problem?" The fact is all of us have some sort of handicap. Some handicaps can be seen but the most destructive handicaps are those that cannot be seen—the mental stumbling blocks that lead to mediocrity and failure.

**Lesson From "The Mick"**

One of the greatest hitters in baseball history is Mickey Mantle. Mantle is remembered as a great home run slugger, but do you also know he struck out more than 1,750 times? In addition, he walked to first base more than 1,750 times. In other words, there were more than 3,500 times he went to home plate and didn't hit the ball. That is the equivalent of seven full seasons where he never had a base hit.

However, Mickey Mantle is not famous for the things that he did not accomplish. He is famous for those he did. But, he never would have hit that many home runs if he hadn't had the courage to step up to the plate. Here's the lesson in the form of a question: If you never get up to bat, how are you going to hit a home run? Furthermore, it is not the misses that count—it is the hits. Learn from your misses but focus on your hits.

A common mindset of the successful is that they have a positive expectancy of success and they are tenacious with their goal setting and planning. I think the important thing to these individuals is the effort they expend and the journey they take. If you never go to bat or get in the ball game, you will never get a hit and most certainly never win the game.

You have a choice. You can live life by design or you can live it by default. It's up to you. Get in the batter's box and strike out a few times. That's okay. Never fear failure. When I make a mistake, I increase my awareness and improve my performance. I refuse to relegate my disappointment and failure to the back of my mind. I purposely move it to the forefront where I can deal with it, work out the kinks, make adjustments, and get back on track. I turn my mistakes into stepping stones toward my goal. I figure if I didn't make a mistake today, I didn't learn much as I could have or should have.

**Goal Setting**

Success or failure is up to you. If you want to be a success and overcome the invisible handicaps detrimental to that success, you need to know that you can do it if you think you can. I overcame a handicap that could have stopped a speeding train. You can too. There are a few steps you need to take to start changing your mindset to one of independence and success. Get a notebook and pen and actually complete these steps rather than just read them and apply them in theory. Make yourself accountable.

1. Decide what you want to do. If you try to be all things to all people, you will fail. You have to find a unique position in life that is an ideal fit for you, by your own terms.

2. Set measurable goals. You need both measurable long-term and short-term goals. Write the goals down. Until you write them down, they do not exist. The list does not have to be daunting or wordy. You know what it will take to achieve your goals. All you are really doing is going through the exercise of writing them down.

3. Define how you will attain those goals. After you write your goals down, determine how you will achieve them. Write a step-by-step plan. Create a road map that clearly defines how you are going to reach your destination. Again, it does not have to be daunting or wordy.

4. Work your plan. As you do the daily activity it takes to accomplish your goals, focus on the daily activity rather than the goal. The analogies of "one step at a time" and "take baby steps" apply. Don't overwhelm yourself. Make your short-term goals obtainable. Mini-successes are as important as major successes.

5. Make adjustments as needed. You will make mistakes and experience failure from time to time. When that happens, do some soul searching. Determine where you went wrong and adjust your approach, but do not allow yourself to become distracted from achieving your goals.

6. As you work your plan, start thinking about ways to give to others. If you cannot give away your money, it owns you. If you do not give yourself and your money to others, you will become self-focused and shallow. Contentment will always elude you. If you could reach out to any cause, what would that be? Write it down and begin thinking about what you would like your contribution to be.

7. Be a mentor to others. There are millions of people who would like to be where you are. Take one or two along for the ride with you. Teach them what you have learned.

## Here's the Question

The question you are now faced with is crucial. *What are you going to do with this information?* Will you be inspired to get in the batter's box and take a swing? Or, will you sit in the bleachers as a spectator? It's up to you. My advice is swing away. Strike out, make adjustments, but enjoy the ride. Life can be a thrilling experience. Wouldn't you like to enjoy it?

One of the nagging questions that appear in the mind of real estate investors is, *Should I jump in and invest or has the window of opportunity closed because I waited too long?*

I've noted that many people never begin investing because they are overcome with fear. Fear prevents many people from ever realizing their dreams. They wake up one day and understand they've exhausted their options and have little time left with which to realize those dreams. But you can avoid that dilemma if you take action. If you are not successful now, then to be successful you need to take action and encourage change.

## Fear of Failure

I was 20 years old when I began investing in real estate. Some of my close friends and co-workers thought I had gone crazy. They knew I didn't have any money, and they thought I was too young. As I aged and continued to invest in real estate, some people laughed still at me and told me I was crazy. Everybody has an opinion—and everyone has a horror story of a friend going broke in real estate.

Rule number one in real estate investing is very simple: don't hang around with negative thinkers. They will fill your head with "what ifs." What if you can't make a monthly payment? What if the economy falls flat? What if you loose all your money? What if you can't rent the house or apartment complex? What if you get sued? What if you can't get the repairs done? The what if's are endless and they can consume your thoughts if you let them.

When I purchased my first property, I didn't know a lot about real estate investing. In the late 60s I read William Nickerson's classic work, *How I Turned $1,000 into A $1,000,000*. From that book, I learned about a formula that made sense to me, and I latched onto the promise of real estate riches. I reread the book, took notes, and jumped in. I reduced my risk some by getting a little education before I took the dive. Maybe I wasn't old enough to know better, but I had no fear of failure. Nickerson had done it so I knew that I could also do it. It was as simple as that.

My wife and I purchased a building lot in Santa Rosa, California, for $5,000 with no money down. Then we borrowed a total of $19,000 to pay off the lot and build our first house, also with no money down. We lived in the house for a year and then sold it for $36,000. After deducting a 6-percent real estate fee, we netted about $14,840—twice what I had earned in my construction job and with far less effort because I hired people to build most of the house. It seemed to me a great way of making a living.

I could have listened to those who thought I was getting in over my head. I could have decided that I was too young—just like some of them said. I could have been wrapped in fear of failure—but wasn't. In my mind, there was no reason not to take the risk. I had nothing to lose.

## Fear of Success

Why do people fear success? Some people feel undeserving of success. They are continually subconsciously sabotaging their dreams, hopes, and desires. They have a recurring negative mental image that takes priority in their thinking. It's what I call negative self-talk. They think they're not worthy or deserving of a good life. And they know it's true because they tell themselves that in countless ways.

You have to replace the negative self-talk with positive affirmations. That's why I insist the members of my real estate investment group identify themselves as real estate investors. I demand that they say, "Hi, I'm so n' so, I'm a real estate investor." I want that statement to become a self-fulfilling prophecy. I want them to understand there is more out there. I want them to capture and enjoy success. I want to lead them from where they are into greater accomplishments. I want them to fulfill their potential.

## Fear of the Unknown

When I was 14 years old, I lived near a bridge that crossed the Russian River. The boys in our town liked to jump from the bridge into the river, and I longed to do the same but the thought terrified me. Even though no one ever got hurt, I was still scared. One day I made up my mind I was going to do it.

I remember that first jump as though it were yesterday. I can still feel the fear that swelled up inside me. I can still feel the wind slapping my face while falling midair. I can still feel the cool water as my feet broke the surface and I plummeted into the depths of the water, my knees buckling when I hit the river bottom. Gasping for air as my head cleared the surface of the water, I had a feeling of success. I had done it. I had proven myself to my peers. In the process, however, I overcame my fear.

After my successful jump it was much easier the second time. It got easier with each additional jump, and eventually I had no fear at all.

In real estate investing, we overcome fear with information. You get information by reading books, having a mentor, taking a class, purchasing a course, attending a boot camp, networking with like-minded people, and through experience.

What is keeping you from jumping in and investing in real estate? What's holding you back and when will you start? At one point I had 26 offers accepted offers to purchase real estate and in escrow. But it would have never happened if I hadn't taken that first plunge into the investment market all those years ago. In summary, this is what you need to do:

1. If you fear failure, get educated and take action. It's the only way to gain power over your fear of failure.

2. If you fear success, define what it is that you want to accomplish and engage in positive self-talk and affirmations.

3. If you fear the unknown, jump in anyway. Jump in and enjoy the exhilaration of success.

In our culture, it is quite common for people to accept their position in life. Oh, they may grumble about politicians, the opportunities their employers may offer, or complain that they don't have any extra money, but few do anything to implement change. You are already ahead of the crowd just by reading this book. You will truly be ahead of the game if you put even one or two principles you are about to learn into practice.

There are many roads to gaining wealth in real estate investing—buying foreclosures or rental units and developing land just a few. Can those opportunities make you money? Yes, it is certainly possible. Allow me to go on to say that it is virtually impossible not to if you follow certain investment rules. I developed a list of rules that apply to any real estate investment prospect. The rules are simple, and I learned them from various mentors over the years. The rules are:

1. Does this opportunity create wealth? In other words, when I close the transaction, did I increase my net worth?

2. How much out-of-pocket expense? In other words, how much of my cash will I have to put into this project?

3. When do I get my money back? In other words, if I have to use my own money, will I get it back in a timely fashion, and if so, when?

4. Does this opportunity create a positive cash flow? In other words, will the deal put money into my pocket or take money out of my pocket?

For now, just understand that is it possible to know for certain that you will make money and create wealth when you conduct a real estate transaction. Without doubt, real estate investing has been the most effective way of creating wealth in our country. Real estate has out performed the stock market, mutual funds, and insurance annuities. Here is a sample of why real estate is so good to us:

1. Leverage. **In real estate, it is possible to invest with no money down.** In general, if you purchase $200,000 in IBM stock, you will pay the full $200,000. If the stock increases 10 percent, you made $20,000. If you purchase a home for $200,000 with no money down and the market goes up 10 percent, you also made $20,000— but you didn't have to put up $200,000 to achieve the same result. And, you had a place to live while your investment appreciated.

2. Demand. **People will always need a place to live.** The simple fact is that our population continues to grow, and the increased population needs to live somewhere. There will always be a need for housing!

3. Tax advantages. **Real estate investors enjoy one of the best tax rates and tax advantages available.** Not only can you get rich, you can have more spendable income derived from rental depreciation. You can erase your tax liability by owning and renting real estate. Be sure to consult your tax advisor on how to accomplish this.

4. Appreciation. **Property values continue to rise.** No other investment offers the same benefit as real estate appreciation when you factor in the fact that you can own and/or control property with little out-of-pocket expense.

5. Passive Income. **If you have little or no money out of pocket invested and you have a steady stream of income, is it possible to quit that 9 to 5 job?** The answer is yes, if you have enough passive income. Will buying stock earn you enough monthly income on which you can live in a manner to which you are accustomed? I do not think so.

6. Increased Value. **If you change the use of a property, you can increase its value.** For example, if you can buy a property and slit off one or more extra building lots, you increased its value. If you offer creative financing (owner carry, land sale contract, carry a second, lease option) you increase its value. If you can have a property rezoned for a better use, you have increased its value. You can, with little or no money, good credit or bad, beat the rat race and break free from that day job that forces you into accepting second best.

Is real estate still a good investment? Let's look at the hard facts. The average real estate investor will accumulate more wealth than the average stock investor will, even though the return on stocks appears to be higher.

How can that happen? The answer to that is leverage. Leverage, as applied here, means the money you borrow increases your power position. The more you leverage, the faster your wealth will grow.

## Do the Math

Which is the better deal? If you purchase $100,000 worth of stock, you have committed $100,000 in cash. Those are dollars that you cannot touch if you want to produce a return on that investment, and what the return might be is questionable. If you purchase $100,000 in real estate, you will have only $10,000 or less out of pocket (10-percent down payment) and you have someone in the house making your payments and building your equity and essentially putting up the "investment cash" on your behalf.

But there is more. You can take cash out of your real estate through loans. You can borrow against the equity and those loan proceeds are not taxable income. Real estate investing allows you, through loans, to take money out of your property for other investments. Think about it.

You can use tax free (or deferred) money to invest in another property, you get to keep the original property, and you have just doubled your investment portfolio. I hope I now have your attention. Anyone can do it—male or female—but only a few will.

# Chapter 2

## Treat Your Business Like a Business

### Getting Started

The first thing you need to do to set yourself up for success is select the appropriate structure for your business. Many businesses of all types fail within the first 5 years because this very important detail is overlooked. We are going to review the types of business structures and what they mean. There is no test at the end of the chapter, and this is not information you need to memorize. This information is provided to give you a brief insight to your business structure options.

If you feel out of your element with this information, you are not alone. Complete books and manuals have been written on this topic alone. No one expects you to understand every detail of every business element. However, some knowledge is better than no knowledge. This chapter is intended to provide you with adequate information to educate yourself enough to ask the appropriate questions to those who know the answers.

### Business Structures

Before you set up a new business structure, be sure to talk with your accountant and attorney. They are the experts, and you should always carefully consider their expertise. You may be wondering why you need a structure at all. That's an excellent question. I am going to make a lengthy, complicated answer brief so you learn only the information you need to move ahead. What follows are the types of business structures and a brief definition of what they are and how they work.

*Sole-Proprietorship.* A sole-proprietorship is the simplest form of business in which a sole owner and his business are not legally distinct entities. The owner is usually liable for business debts.

*General Partnership.* A general partnership is a partnership in which there are no limited partners, and each partner has managerial power and untitled liability for partnership debts.

*Limited Partnership.* A limited partnership has limited and general partners. The general partners manage the business and are individually liable for the debts of the partnership. The limited partners are limited in the amount they can lose by the amount of money they invested in the partnership.

*S-Corporation.* A corporation is eligible to be taxed under the subchapter S of the Internal Revenue Code. Basically, shareholders pay tax on the corporation's income by reporting their prorate shares of pass-through items on their own individual income tax returns.

*Corporation.* A corporation is an organization authorized by state law to act as a legal entity distinct from its owners. A corporation has its own name and has its own powers to achieve legal purposes, and is, therefore, a separate legal entity.

*Limited Liability Company (LLC).* The Limited Liability Company (LLC) is a hybrid between a corporation and a limited partnership. LLCs provide protection from personal liability, just as corporations do, and yet LLCs receive the tax treatment of limited partnerships, or a C corporation, whichever the members of the LLC desire. The best structure for building business credit is one that will separate you from your business and separates the debts of the business from that of the owner or officers. Your business should have its own tax identification number so that you can build business credit thus reducing your risk of an Internal Revenue Service audit. The business structures that best meet that criterion are S Corporation, C Corporation, and LLC. So, let's break down these three a little further.

Consider an *S Corporation* if the owners live in a state with no personal state income tax, one or two individuals own the company (can be as many as 35), and has sales less than $250,000.

Consider a *C Corporation* if the owners live outside the country, live in a state with a state income tax, and/or if several individuals or other entities are involved in the ownership, and sales are greater than $60,000.

Consider a *Limited Liability Company* if you are in a partnership, have several entities that own the business, the owners have real estate for investment purposes, and if the owner is looking for complete protection of their personal liability. You may find that you will want to open a couple business structures for distinct purposes as your business grows and progresses. Many advantages can result in having an in-depth knowledge of the business structures and how you can use them to further your independence. Let's go over LLCs a little further because that is likely the first type of business structure into which you will enter. Remember, this is not advice to enter into an LLC. You should contact your accountant and attorney for advice specific to your situation.

### Limited Liability Company (LLC)

How can you grow your business and use the LLC umbrella? I suggest that you set up a stand-alone LLC for each property. If you own 10 properties in one LLC and you get sued, all 10 properties are potentially at risk. If you own 10 properties under 10 separate LLCs, your risk is limited to only 1 property.

Personally, I don't have significant assets in any one company, nor do I have any property in my name. While not appreciated by some attorneys, the approach does limit my exposure to lawsuits. It also cuts down on my legal bills. In addition, if you are sued, as a real estate investor you are virtually out of business. The title company will check public records before a loan is closed and when they find that pending suit, with you as the defendant, they will not approve financing. Without a loan, you can't fund your projects. For a real estate investor that is a death sentence.

Having endured a frivolous lawsuit, I can attest to the fact that it is best to get assets out of your name. The lesson cost me about $30,000 in fees and legal costs, even though the suit was settled in my favor. In essence, it cost me $30,000 plus countless hours of anxiety and study to learn how to protect myself in future litigation. I am providing the education I obtained through experience to you now.

For several years I operated a business in a wrong business structure. Not knowing any better, I foolishly operated as a sole-proprietor. That meant that everything I owned was available to anyone who wanted to sue me.

Everything was at risk, including my family's home. Things have changed over the years and I am a little wiser about business. I am sharing this information with you so you can learn from my mistakes and save yourself the losses of those mistakes as a result.

**Everyone Should Own a Business—Let Me Tell You Why**

**First**, if you own a business you are already a step ahead of the crowd. You can enjoy tax advantages that most people you know can't, unless they too, have a business. In real terms, that means you have more spendable money. You can start writing off several expenses, including vacations, with before-tax dollars.

How you would like to be able to do that? If done correctly, it is doable.

**Second**, if your plan is to quit your day job and become a full-time investor, you can more easily qualify for traditional financing if you've been in business for 2 years. It matters little that you didn't make much money. What matters is your Certified Public Accountant can write a letter stating you've been in business.

**Third**, if you have your own business you can set up a self-directed 401k retirement plan when appropriate. The reason that's important is you can loan money from your 401K (charged points and fees) and buy property in that retirement account name while deferring or eliminating taxes on the growth of the fund. You can amass huge sums of money quickly and pay lower taxes at the same time if done properly, all of the time gaining protection for your property under a corporation or LLC. That is the short list. There are many advantages you have when you form a company.

**How Do I Set Up a New Business?**

I have talked about the importance of protecting your personal assets and separating them through an appropriate business structure, and I have mentioned some other great advantages to being self-employed that clock-punching employees do not have. Hopefully, the information has not been too boring. Remember, you don't need to be an expert in law or accounting, but it is always important to know enough to be able to ask the right questions to the experts.

You now have a pretty good understanding of the foundation of starting your own business. Now, you just need to execute. This is what you need to do next.

***Step One.*** Decide what business you want to operate.

*Step Two.* Decide on a business structure. Talk to your attorney and tax advisor about the type of business structure best for you. I think most new businesses should do well if they are set up as an LLC. An LLC will fundamentally give you the protection of a corporation while treating income more favorably than a corporation will.

*Step Three.* Choose a name. Give serious thought to the name you use. Make yourself a list of the possibilities. When you have weighed all the pros and cons and have a "short list" left, you need to find out if that name is available for use. Search your state government website to determine how to check if the name is available.

*Step Four.* Once you decide on a company name, you must register the name with the state. Every state has different forms for registering a business name. Locate the website for your state government, locate the search field, and locate the field to register your business name. Follow the instructions. While there, search through other new business information on their site. If you intend to do business across multiple states or across the country, you may want to consider filing your company's name with the federal government.

*Step Five.* You need a federal employer identification number (EIN) for banking purposes. It's very easy to obtain. You can also use your Social Security Number, but getting an EIN is easy and if you do any business at all you will need one at some point. So, go ahead and get it now. Go to http://www.irs.gov/ where you can either proceed with the online application, which is very easy, or call the 800 number. If you call, they are very friendly and helpful. They will give you an EIN while you are on the phone. Be sure to write it down and keep it safe.

*Step Six.* You now need a LLC Operating Agreement. You can get your attorney's advice and have him prepare the document. You can also purchase a prepared one at one of the local office supply or specialty bookstores, or you can also borrow one from a friend and retype it. In any event, you need an agreement that describes how you will operate your business. If you are setting up an LLC for the first time, spend the money and talk to an attorney. It will be money well spent. Be sure to have annual meetings so you fulfill the LLC requirement. You don't want a judge later on declaring your LLC a shell and not really a business as a result of a minor oversight.

Now you have the basic steps in setting up your company. One final thought . . . why not take your spouse to Maui for your Annual Meeting next year? You can do that and write part of the cost off your income tax. Isn't that great?

**Protecting Your Assets With a Revocable Living Trust**

For each property I purchase, I create a Land Trust and deed the property to the trust. I do that for two reasons. First, it makes it very easy to put some real estate transactions together without violating the "Due on Sale" clause found in normal trust deeds, and second, it helps protect my assets.

A Revocable Trust is a document through which wealthy people hold property in an attempt to avoid taxes and attorney fees after death. Through the trust, they are able to pass on their real or personal property to others. It is an 8- to 12-page document describing the details of the duties and responsibilities of all the parties to the trust.

A Revocable Trust can also be used by the not so wealthy to shield property ownership and create and hold wealth. Because the names of beneficiaries of a trust are private information, the trust provides a degree of safety and personal privacy. In today's litigious society where personal information is readily available, the Trust can result in fewer lawsuits.

Having a trust does not mean you can't be sued but it does make the possibility less likely. To add personal protection, you can form an LLC or a Corporation for each property owned and name it as the Trust beneficiary. The advantage of that is if you are sued because of an alleged injury on one property and the plaintiff prevails, your loss is limited to that property rather than all properties owned.

An attorney once suggested to me that I deed a property to a LLC or Corporation at the point of purchase and forego the trust. However, I prefer the Revocable Trust because federal law prohibits a lender from accelerating the note if ownership changes when the property is deeded to the trust. This is not the case when properties are deeded to a Limited Liability Company or Corporation.

A further benefit comes when you decide to sell your property. You can sell your beneficial interest in the property with a simple, private, one-page transfer of beneficial interest. You can also sell on a Land Sales Contract (also called an installment land contract or contract for deed). In fact, with a Revocable Living Trust, several possibilities become available to you for an exit strategy.

**Stay in Business**
If a plaintiff files suit and your method of operation is to secure loans from traditional sources, your real estate investing days are over for a period of time—perhaps even a few years. When a suit is filed, that suit is public record. Imagine that you have three deals in escrow and have credit scores over 750 (very good credit risk). Before you sign the closing documents, the title company runs a final check and they discover you are being sued. Guess what happens? Your lenders refuse to loan you the money and your deals fall through.

If your property is in a trust, your trustee is served papers, which means there will be no public record you are a party to a lawsuit. In such a case, you can close your loans and continue in business. Granted, the first time you read through this information it will sound slightly complicated. Break it up in sections and read it again until it does make sense. It's very important to have this knowledge so you know how to protect you and your business.

### Private Property
You can also use a trust to hold private property. You can place your vehicles in a trust, your antique furniture, you plasma television, your coin collection, silver and gold bullion—whatever you own. Legally you own nothing, but you still retain the beneficial interests in and use of those possessions. If someone attempts to go after you in a lawsuit, holding your property in trust makes it very difficult for anyone to obtain anything.

### How Do I Set Up a Trust?
One option I recommend is to talk to a good estate planning attorney who understands real estate. He will be worth his weight in gold. Make sure he understands what you want to accomplish and have him draw up the documents. I had my attorney e-mail me a copy of the trust documents so I could use the forms again when I set up new trusts. He taught me what I needed to know by walking through the first one with me. Now, all I have to do in fill in the new information.

Another option is to purchase a course on the subject. Attorney Bill Bronchick, has a course you can purchase at www.LegalWiz.com. In that course he gives you information about setting up a trust as well as the documents you need for completing one. I personally have completed the course and recommend it.

A third option is to purchase blank forms. There are companies on line and in storefronts that sell documents. Simply fill in the blanks and file a Bargain and Sale Deed (or perhaps a Quit Claim Deed – check with your title company) with the county recorder. If you choose that route, discuss the trust documents with your attorney to make sure they are legal in your state.

**More about Trusts**

The parties to the trust include a grantor (someone who deeds the property to the trustee), a grantee (the trustee who has full authority to act on the behalf of those who have beneficial interest), and a beneficiary (anyone who enjoys the benefit of the trust). I suggest having someone other than you serve as trustee for your own trust. I have several trusts, and I am not the trustee of any (this drives my estate planning attorney nuts, but he deals with it.)

You might want a trusted relative or a friend in another state to serve as the trustee. At one point I listed a friend in Colorado as the trustee in one of my trusts and used a local address for him. My reasoning: if he was difficult to find, the process of serving him with legal documents would be extremely difficult and perhaps remote.

When I use a trust to purchase property, I use the name of the seller. At the time of closing they sign all the trust documents including an addendum (not public information) making me co-trustee (I'm the beneficiary) with all the rights to sign any trust related documents. Such a strategy might be a gold mine for you if you use it correctly.

Remember that there are many layers to the legalities of real estate investing. I am educating you, very briefly, on some of the things you will want to learn more about so that you can use the benefits available to you in your business. If you do not know about them, you might not ask about them, and they might not be offered by another party. So refer to these details as you establish the legalities of your business with your attorney.

**After the Paperwork Is Done**

When your trust is complete, file the trust documents in a safe place at your home or office. That document and related addendums are for your private use only. You will only need them when you have some trust related business to perform. Once you set up your trusts, you can go to bed and sleep better knowing you have taken some steps to protect your hard-earned wealth.

**The Layers of Real Estate Investing**

As previously discussed, the layers of real estate investing run very deep. They involve sellers, buyers, real estate agents, lenders, title companies, loan officers, mortgage brokers, accountants, and attorneys. If you enter into the business of real estate investing and you take away only one thing, let it be this: *you are not the expert at every level and you need to locate resources that are.* You need to build yourself a team of people upon whom you can rely and who will also benefit as your business grows.

Below is a flowchart that shows the layers of real estate investing, how those layers tie together, and what the big picture looks like. This flow chart does not capture every detail but should give you a snapshot of the process.

**Establishing Goals and Preparing a Business Plan**

You are probably not surprised to hear that you are going to need a business plan if you want to keep your business alive and thriving. You may have been under the impression, however, that business plans are for big companies and not for the small company yours is going to be when you start out. The reality is that thought couldn't be further from the truth.

Because your business is small is an even greater reason to have a business plan. "Plan the work and work the plan" is a proverb essential to the success of any business, especially so if you're a start up. The last thing you want to do is run yourself ragged on things that don't have an impact on your annual goals.

A business plan puts everything you do for your business into perspective. If you're spending too much time on something and it does not directly contribute to your business objectives, you know it is time not well spent.

And vice versa, if that is the case. Having a business plan is about always knowing and understanding what the path to success is and exactly how you will get there. Like a lot of things I already covered, this topic may seem overwhelming, but your first business plan does not have to be beautiful and publisher perfect.

As a matter of fact, the plan can be written on a tablet of paper where the changes you make are crossed out with pen or pencil. The purpose of a business plan is to force you to think through your goals, how you're going to achieve those goals, and to make the commitment to yourself by putting it in writing. A business plan is an excellent "big picture" tool that aids you in taking a step back and making sure that the details haven't forced you off track.

A business plan is also about measurement. You should, on a regular basis, evaluate the success of your time, your tactics, and your objectives. Changing your business plan is fine. But having a plan and incorporating changes is a checks and balances for objectives. Ask yourself why you are making a particular change and what you learned that changed the direction of your business. Are your objectives still realistic? If they aren't, change them. The last thing you want is an unrealistic business plan that serves more as a punishment than a tool for success.

Included below is a sample outline of a business plan. There are probably thousands of variations of business plan templates and "How to" books available. The trick to sticking to the plan is writing the plan so it makes sense. If portions of the following plan or the template you choose do not apply to your business, then don't use them.

That doesn't mean you can skip the parts you don't want to do. Force yourself to commit to your goals and objectives and how you plan to achieve them. I have seen business plans that include the tactical day-to-day practices. I believe that is probably overkill, but you should at least consider how the plan affects you all the way down to hours per day.

You will also need to do the financial portion of your business plan. I realize that you are still learning some of the methods that you will be using to purchase new properties, but it's important you have an understanding of what the expectations are, so that as you learn, you can make changes with a purpose.

This first part below is a questionnaire designed to direct your thoughts toward completion of the actual business plan. The questionnaire contains questions you will likely need to answer to fill out the business plan as completely and comprehensively as possible. The questionnaire is designed to be a tool to help you with the business plan. You don't have to use it, or you can use it on a very limited basis, but hopefully it will stir productive thoughts that you may have overlooked. The business plan outline that follows the questionnaire is typical for a start-up business. If you want to get to Emerald City, you need to follow the yellow brick road. Consider your plan your yellow brick road.

Part I
Business Plan Questionnaire
    1. What is the name of your business? What is your address? What is your contact information?
        1.1. Do you have a Web site?
        1.2. Why do you want to start this business?
        1.3. Provide a brief history.
    2. What are your goals or objectives?

3. Do you have a mission statement?

4. Have you determined a corporate structure?

5. Clearly describe the nature of your business.

    5.1. Does it require a license of any type?

    5.2. Is it seasonal or otherwise impacted?

6. Explain in detail your product(s) or service(s).

7. Describe your customer.

    7.1. Business customer

    7.2. Individual customer

8. Who are your competitors?

    8.1. Is there a company with a similar business model?

9. How does your competition promote itself?

10. What advantages do you have over your competition?

11. What disadvantages do you have compared with your competition?

12. What is your unique advantage?

13. How long do you anticipate the start-up phase of this business to take?

14. When do you plan to launch?

15. What other parties will be promoting your business?

16. Should your service, product, or site be patented? Can it be?

17. How do you intend to market your business?

18. What technological capacities do you have in place? (Web specific expertise.)

    18.1. Will they track site statistics?

    18.2. Will they provide 24-hour support/reliability?

    18.3. What pieces are internal?

    18.4. What pieces are outsourced?

    18.5. What hardware or software do you need for your site?

18.6. Briefly describe front-end technology and backend technology.

18.7. What is the shelf life of this type of technology? When will it need replacing?

18.8. Who will design and build your site?

18.9. What is the flow chart of your site?

18.10. What is the time line associated with this flow chart?

18.11. Do you have a chat room?

18.12. Do users need to sign in?

19. Where do you see your business in 6 months, 1 year, 3 years, and 5 years?

20. Does your structure allow for growth?

21. Are there any growth limitations with your plan?

22. Do you have a brick and mortar business (storefront)?

23. Do you have an attorney?

24. Do you have an accountant?

25. Who is your management team? (Brief profiles with specific strengths and experience.)

26. Who is your outside consultant team? (If you have one/them.)

27. What equipment do you need?

28. What will that equipment cost?

29. What other inventory do you need?

30. What do you anticipate your total start-up costs are? How much capital are you looking for? Itemize your start-up costs.

31. Provide a brief description of your financial picture.

32. Do you have a profit and loss statement? What financial software will you use?

33. What type of borrowing structure are you looking for?

34. How will your investors (venture capital structure) receive a return on their investment? (if applicable)

35. Provide a brief description of what the capital will be used for.

36. Do you have any controlling interests in other businesses?

37. Is this business an extension of any other businesses?

38. Do you have any supporting documents to solidify your claims to the investor or lender?

39. Are you a member of any associations that have statistical or factual information?

40. Have you already done any preliminary research to support your objectives?

41. What sources have been the best for collecting information specific to your business?

Part II
Business Plan Outline

Cover Sheet
Table of Contents
1) Executive Summary
    a) Overview
        (1) Statement of Purpose - brief
    b) Context of your business
        i) The market, your customers, your product or service
        ii) Objectives
            (a) Understand what you want and need to accomplish
    c) Start-Up Summary
        i) A Snapshot of your situation
        ii) Calculation of ratio and quick ratio (optional)
        iii) Anticipated challenges and planned responses
        iv) Company ownership (such as LLC or partnership)
2) Products and Services
    a) Description of your product or service) Web site Plan—assume we are talking to people who do not use the Internet, not too deep, but highly informative
        (1) Content outline
        (2) Content details
        (3) Unique position
        (4) Site reliability
        (5) Technical support
            (a) Host, domain, software solutions – brief
        (6) Ease of use
    b) Added value
    c) Competitive edge
    d) Tests or proven examples
    e) Lifecycle

f) Trademarks and copyrights

g) Keys to Success—what will make or break this business

3) Market Analysis Summary (Macro Overview)

    a) Market segmentation

        i) Reliable statistical information

        ii) Market strengths and weaknesses

        iii) Customer profile

        iv) Competition

    b) Target Market Segment Strategy

4) Strategy and Implementation Summary

    a) SWOT (strength, weakness, opportunities, threats) analysis

        i) Strengths

        ii) Weaknesses

        iii) Opportunities

        iv) Threats

    b) Sales and Marketing Strategy

        i) Marketing Strategy

            (1) Build a Marketing Plan—to pull the surfer in

                (a) SEO, keywords, and Meta tags, linking strategies and Web directories with focus on reaching that demographic through Google, MSN Search, and Yahoo.

                (b) Effective on-line advertising strategy evaluating banner ads, pay per click and e-mail newsletters. Offline (or cross-promotion) advertising?

                (c) Concise e-mail marketing message and format of an opt-in e-mail list in compliance with the CAN SPAM Act.

                (d) Public relations opportunities that appeal to target audience (where is the free exposure?).

                (e) Affiliate marketing on-line programs including effectiveness, with pros and con's.

                (f) On-line community to build brand awareness and repeat clients (to blog or not to blog).

      ii) Sales Strategy—pulling the advertiser in
         (1) Selling Tactics
            (a) Affiliate marketing
            (b) Traditional targeting, prospecting
         (2) Sales Forecast
   c) Milestones
      i) Time frames
      ii) Checks and balances strategy
5) Management Summary
   a) Personnel Plan
      i) Chart your formal organization
      ii) Management team introduction
      iii) People and talent requirements
         (1) Outsource?
         (2) Legal
         (3) Technical
         (4) Financial
         (5) Other
      iv) Compensation
6) Financial Plan
   a) Start-up funding
   b) Important assumptions
      i) Financial projections
      ii) Implementation schedule
      iii) Statement of resource needs
   c) Break-even analysis
      i) The number one question all investors ask: "When will I get a return on my investment?"
   d) Projected profit and loss
   e) Projected cash flow
   f) Projected balance sheet
7) Summary

a) Support
    i) Provide supporting documents and sources for statistical claims
  b) Call to Action
  c) Appendix

Your completed business plan is intended to be used, not simply put in a binder and put on a shelf somewhere as a decoration. Once you complete the plan, it will be a great tool when working with lenders and loan officers. They are, after all, kind of like partners in your business and when working with them you should "sell" your plan to them so they understand that you understand what it means to run a business. Their perceived risk is much less if you can show them where the return on their investment is coming from and more importantly, when they will get it.

**Your Duty to Yourself and Your New Business**
Henry Ford once said: "If you think education is expensive, try ignorance." That's a true saying. The cost of education is a lot less than learning by trial and error. The cost of a seminar can be repaid in one transaction that you wouldn't have been able to do without the information.

I've seen real estate investors stumble along for years without making any money because they lack education. Some feel they have more knowledge than the experts do, some lack the patience to gain an education, and others just don't want to spend the time and money needed to educate themselves. Such attitudes usually lead to costly mistakes.

One common denominator between most new real estate investors is their failure to see the importance of spending money on their education. Rather than sign up for a coaching program or attend seminars that seem too expensive, they opt for increasing their education through books or free seminars.

Reading books is great. I read a lot of books. But I have yet to find one book with all the information I need on real estate investing. Even the best authors have a blind spot or two in their books. Those types of blind spots can leave critical gaps in your education if you depend solely on books for your information. Regarding investment seminars, my experience is that you generally get what you pay for.

For example, I attended a weekend seminar with Bill Bronchick, a Colorado attorney, writer, and real estate investor. I paid about $2,000 for the event, plus airfare and hotel accommodations. "That's a lot of money!" my wife complained. I had to agree, but I felt the information it promised would benefit me. The result? I took the information I gained from that one weekend of education and within a few months netted $1,200,000. The cost of the information was well worth the investment, and my wife no longer complains about the cost of seminars.

Will everyone have that kind of a return? Probably not, but if you take the information you learn and apply it, you will more than cover the cost of your investment. You must educate yourself if you want to earn significant sums of money. Here's what you need to do:

**1. Read lots of books and articles.** The more you read, the better you will understand concepts and principles. Allow time in your daily schedule for reading.

**2. Attend seminars**. The real estate investment industry has many seminars and boot camps. Attend as many as you can. Some are better than others. Invest with the best, and you will make money faster. If you are a professional investor, the costs of attending are tax deductible.

**3. Hire an investment coach or mentor**. They can help you avoid common mistakes and steer you in a profitable direction more quickly by tracking your real estate investment career. Money spent here is money well spent in most cases.

**4. Take an online investment course.** Many real estate investment Web sites offer free courses that will help you gain the knowledge you need. I think the best Web site for good, sound information at affordable prices is www.LegalWiz.com.

**5. Realize that education takes time and will not happen over night.** You have to learn to crawl before you walk and walk before you run. Wisdom comes after you've gained your education and begin applying what you've learned.

**6. Join a local Real Estate Investment Club.** You will have the opportunity to learn from seasoned veterans, and you will find like-minded people from whom you can learn important lessons. One of the best parts of my investment club is the encouragement the investors receive each week from fellow investors.

**7. Learn how to give.** Become a mentor yourself. Realize that not everyone has your level of knowledge. Invite someone who knows less than you do to come along with you for the ride. As you mentor them you will learn lessons, too.

# Chapter 3

# Financing Your Business
## Conventional Financing Options

Although conventional financing is an option for real estate investments, for several reasons it is typically not the first type sought. By definition, conventional financing is any loan not eligible for federal insurance or guaranteed by a government agency. Examples of government agencies are Housing and Urban Development (HUD), Government National Mortgage Association (GNMA), Federal Housing Association (FHA), Veterans Administration (VA), and the Farmers Home Administration (FmHA).

The various programs are required to meet the guidelines of Fannie Mae or Freddie Mac and sometimes referred to as conforming loans. The most obvious guideline limitation is the maximum loan limit Fannie Mae and Freddie Mac and adjusted each year to account for the change in average home sales prices nationwide. Government-sponsored and monitored programs typically have a required laundry list of criteria before financing can be approved. As with most government-managed processes, securing financing for one of these programs often takes longer than conventional loans approved only by the bank providing the financing.

Many types of conventional loan programs are available. The programs include fixed rate, adjustable rate (ARM), balloon, biweekly, and convertible. In addition to the types of conventional loans, loan programs also offer a variety of approval criteria and features. The terms, loan-to-value, varying income, no-income-verification, and various credit score requirements, are just a few variables given different levels of consideration to achieve the desired outcome. In other words, loan officers have more to work with in conventional lending situations when seeking approval and to sell you or your business on your behalf.

Real estate investment loans are not always considered conventional. As a result, you are not given the same terms as someone buying the home to reside in. Buying investment property for rental purposes, or to renovate and sell again, is considered a commercial investment and commercial loan terms apply. Many of the residential loan approval criteria are also applicable for commercial loan approval and consideration as well.

Much like residential mortgage loans, different banks offer programs and packages for their commercial lenders. Always do your homework before you accept loan terms from any one institution. Ask about the difference between conventional residential and commercial. Ask about programs specific to your type of business. If you ask enough of the right questions, banks may then begin to offer more information than they otherwise would have. Most loan officers are paid in a salary-plus commission structure. They want to secure financing for you, however, they may also be motivated to sell you loan programs that offer them a higher commission. So, be sure to ask enough of the right questions so they present all of the options.

Ultimately, the decision for loan approval comes from a higher power than the loan officer. The decision will come from either a local board or a corporate underwriting department. If you are working with a involved loan program, the decision for approval comes from the sponsoring government program.

Don't give out your Social Security Number or your business identification number to every loan officer you talk with. There is truth to the fact that every time a credit check is run against your Social Security Number it pulls your credit rating down.

**Creative Financing Options** "No money down," exclaimed the naysayer, "you can't do that. It's not ethical." Many people watch the "How to Buy Real Estate" infomercials on late night and weekend television and see slick productions and pitchmen promising riches beyond belief if only the viewer will use their credit card and call in. In fairness, there is some solid information being offered (sometimes, I watch them, too).

There is a lot of hype from folks who make their money selling expensive programs and boot camps. If you purchase their program, you have to have the tenacity and discipline to read the materials and follow their prescribed formula to make a go of it. But let's get to the real question: Can you really buy real estate with no money down? The answer is, yes!

People have been led to believe it's impossible to purchase property without using your own cash. However, I've been doing it successfully since the late 1970s when I was forced to simply to survive. Much of what I know is a direct result of the real estate depression (not a slow down or recession) in Bend, Oregon, which began at that time and ran through the mid-1980s.

Things were not pretty— but I learned a lot of valuable lessons during that time. I regularly purchase with little or no cash out of my pocket. In fact, at one time I closed a $5,500,000 real estate purchase without using my own money. In addition, I actually received a check at the end of closing. I almost never buy a house if I have to pay money out of pocket.

Perhaps the more important question is: Can you afford 100-percent financing and still enjoy cash flow? Even if you could secure a 100% loan, would that be a good idea? The answer is: Maybe, Maybe not. It depends on your strategy. At this point I will say that 100% financing may not be a good thing.

Here's some important questions for your to consider. I know I mentioned it earlier, but it is worth mentioning again. I teach my protégées to ask four questions when entering into a real estate purchase:

1. Does this purchase create wealth today?
2. How much money out of my pocket will this transaction take?
3. When do I get that money back?
4. Does this project have a positive cash flow? If you have positive answers to these questions, you may have a good deal. Before you spend your hard-earned money for a dream of real estate riches, here is a list of ways to purchase with no money down.

**Talk to Your Lender**

One member of your success team should be a lender with whom you regularly do business. Call that team member and ask about zero down loan programs. There are now several options available to you—especially if you are a first time homebuyer. There are also FHA and federal VA loans that are very close to zero down. It is possible to get an 80-percent loan-to-value first mortgage and a 20-percent second, but be careful. The monthly payments may be too expensive to justify the purchase. It is imperative you run an investment analysis for each property you consider for purchase. The truth is in the numbers, and your lender will be pleased to see that you get that, even before you talked to them. If you can prove through your analysis that it is a wise investment, that will go a long way to achieving success in securing a loan.

**Home Equity Line of Credit -- (HELOC)**

At this writing HELOCS are a thing of the past. One thing I used to do was carry a Home Equity Line of Credit (called HELOC) on each rental I own. Then if cash is needed to close a deal I can write a check from the account. I had more than $600,000 in credit lines from my HELOC loans. One bank has gave me a credit card tied to my HELOC with a credit line of $99,999.

You should, however, use caution when using a line of credit. The first thing I ask myself before drawing money from a HELOC is, when will I get this money back to pay off the loan? If you can't answer that question, do not borrow the money. Any cash advance will increase your monthly payments.

Also make sure you are not upside down with your cash flow. That is a common mistake of many new investors. The financial analysis you prepare before you purchase a property shouldn't be sweetened in any way to make the deal look better on paper than it really is. If you can't achieve cash flow or a reasonable return on your investment, find a different property.

**Seller Financing**

Don't overlook the possibility of the seller lending you the down payment. If you are marketing and talking to the right sellers – specifically motivated ones, they may well help you get your first mortgage by loaning you enough money to close the deal. I frequently use that technique.

I have had a seller loan me as much as $500,000 with no interest for the first 6 months. I then made sure I turned the property over before 6 months. By the way, the $500,000 could just as easily be $1,000,000 on the right deal. If the seller has a lot of equity or is in foreclosure, creative options are available.

## Raise the Price and Lower the Terms

If you offer the seller more than he is asking, you may be able to pull this one off. He has to be willing to accept the down payment in the form of a note if the house appraises well enough to justify the price increase.

For example, a seller is asking $250,000 for his house with a $15,000 down payment and he is willing to carry the balance of $235,000. You offer him $255,000, or more, in the form of a promissory note instead of cash. He gets a little more return for the extra risk involved. Use your imagination. That's the only thing that restricts your success.

## Use Your Investment Property Inventory

On occasion, I borrowed against another property I own. I currently have a note and trust deed on an investment property that I used instead of cash. That meant I didn't have to come up with dollars to close the deal and gives me tremendous flexibility. Imagine what is possible if you don't always have to borrow the money for your down payment.

## Find an Investor

One trick I teach my protégées is to search for successful people who want to be real estate investors but do not have the time to spend on research. They have the cash and financial strength to do a deal so you help out by supplying the time it takes to locate and negotiate the purchase.

I have several protégées who are in a position to make $100,000 to $500,000 each year without using their cash or credit. They will not do a deal unless there is at least $30,000 total profit in the transaction. Their share in that size of profit is $15,000. This is a great way to get started as an investor. You provide the work and expertise and let your partner supply the money and credit.

## Use Your Commission

If you are a real estate broker/agent, use your commission to get what you want. I use mine when I purchase real estate such as single-family homes, duplexes, bare land, or subdivisions. On one transaction alone I made $350,000 this year. The seller told me what price he wanted, and I added my commission to it.

On single-family homes, using your own commission works well when you are dealing with a For Sale by Owner (FSBO). I have added to their asking price a fee of 3 percent for closing costs and 7 percent for a sales commission I then used on the down payment. Again, be creative.

## Lease Option

If you have never done a lease option, also called to as a Rent-To-Own, you owe it to yourself to start. There are several great reasons to lease option. Some argue that it's best to control rather than own. This is especially true if you have poor credit and you can't, or won't, find a financial partner.

You can negotiate leases with landlords who want to stop being a landlord or an owner and who can't sell a house. Negotiate a small down payment ($100?) but be sure that the payment, or a portion of it, is deducted from the sales price. You should maintain the right to sublease. If possible, make sure your monthly payment is below current rents, then offer to sell the property on a lease option at a higher price than you negotiated, with $5,000 down in the form of option consideration. Then charge an extra $100 to $200 per month in order for you to realize positive cash flow.

## Trade for It

Another technique is to offer the seller something they might need or want. Cash is not the only form of payment. I have traded many times for down payments. Possibilities include such things as boats, cars, recreational vehicles, tractors, gemstones, silver or gold, or personal services. Discover what the seller really wants and offer it for trade.

## Your Family and Friends

You may be able to borrow the money you need from your family, friends, or business partner, but I urge you to be fair and honest with them. Many friendships and family relationships have been strained or lost because of a bad business deal. You may want to offer them a portion of the profit when the property is sold. If they are willing to loan you money, nurture the relationship so you will have the opportunity to borrow again if needed.

If you learn to invest in real estate without using your own hard-earned cash, you will realize returns that can exceed 1,000 percent at a time when many think a 10 percent or 50 percent return is good. If you have money in the bank, I have a challenge for you; on your next real estate transaction, think outside the box and do not use any of your own money. It will open up a whole new world for you.

## Your Credit Rating

I now want to turn your attention to credit. There are many real estate gurus who tell us we don't need good credit to make millions of dollars in the real estate market. While that is certainly true, and I have shown many investors how that can be done, with good credit you can make much more.

Poor credit is a weight around your neck that can kill many good deals. It limits your alternatives and options when the money market dries up. Besides, it is a reflection of your character. A person who isn't faithful paying their monthly bills is a person whose word is not very believable.

The person with "challenged" credit, as we sometimes generously say, has a flashing neon sign on his back that declares: "I know I promised to pay, and I had good intentions, but I decided to buy a new car and take my wife to dinner instead."

Here is what I suggest:

**1. Run a credit report** and make a list of your debts. This will identify who you have to pay and when you should pay.

**2. Don't roll your debt into a credit card and then another.** While this may seem like the answer to your problem, you are only creating a larger monster to deal with later.

**3. Prioritize your credit list.** When facing our financial problems, my wife and I had to work hard to get back to square one. We took the following:

a. We listed our creditors and chose to pay off the ones with the least amount of balance while making minimum payments to the others.

b. When the first debt was paid off, we took the amount we were paying and applied it to the next one on the list.

c. We repeated the process until we were paying large amounts each month to the final credit card.

d. We changed our lifestyle. We rarely ate out; we drove used cars and took low-cost family vacations only if we could do it without using our credit card. My wife shopped for bargains and clipped vendor coupons. It was difficult but well worth it to get back on our feet.

**4. Use credit cards sparingly,** keep low balances and pay on time. Some writers advise us to destroy our credit cards once they are paid in full. I think it's better to keep them and use them carefully to show the credit reporting agencies that you use credit wisely. In that way you can rebuild your credit rating, making available more options to fund your real estate purchases.

**5. Establish a realistic monthly budget** and stick to it. It's the only way to get out of debt and rehabilitate your credit.

**6. Be extremely careful with the equity in your home**. You don't want to draw out your equity and pay off your debt if you have not cured the problem. I've seen many people get into debt, refinance their home (or get a Home Equity Line of Credit), and spend their equity while not addressing the real issue of uncontrollable spending.

**7. There are many resources available to help you overcome your indebtedness so use them**. It has been said, "The more you learn, the more you earn." That is true with regard to building a good credit rating. Use these basic steps to start immediately paying down your debts. You will have many more nights of sound sleep knowing that the phone is not going to ring with a collector at the other end wanting his money. As a bonus, you will be able to get more real estate under contract, and closed, as more avenues of finance open for you based on a strong credit rating.

**Watch Out for Pitfalls**

With the slowing real estate market, some real estate investors are trying to survive financially by refinancing their investment properties, hoping to generate enough cash to keep their heads above water. While that approach may simply serve as a bandage, unless the underlying problem is addressed, the short-term solution could lead to a financially devastating crisis.

There is a widely held real estate investment doctrine that suggests the best way to purchase real estate is maximize the loan amount (over finance it) to get the transaction closed and move on. That is advocated for two reasons. First, it allows for a zero-down approach to investing and second, it can generate cash.

While I believe those two reasons may be valid, they are only insofar as the transaction merits it. The approach works if you are buying significantly below the current market value or if appreciation is rocketing into the stratosphere. In the case of the latter, you should be warned that at some point the rocket always runs out of fuel and crashes back on earth. Take care the rocket doesn't hit you on its downward plummet.

**Smart real estate investors resist the temptation to over finance property simply for the sake of generating cash. They have at least three reasons for this.**

### *Reason #1*

It's best not to over finance your property because you pay a premium if you exceed 80 percent of the value to the loan amount. Historically, lenders embraced the notion that if their investment (loan) is at that value, or less, the risk is acceptable. If the loan value is more than 80 percent, the loan gets more risky for the lender. That is why PMI (Private Mortgage Insurance) exists. PMI ensures that in the event of a default, the lender will not be liable for a loss in excess of 80 percent.

There is another way to accomplish the same thing. You can get a second mortgage (a note and Deed of Trust) on the property for the amount needed above 80 percent. The interest rate will be higher than the first mortgage, and in some cases much higher, but at least it is tax deductible. There have been some recent proposed changes to the tax deductibility of PMI. Be sure to talk to your mortgage broker before you make a final decision on whether to secure a second mortgage or use PMI.

If you happen to find a 100-percent loan, be forewarned— the payment will eat you alive. The high interest rate charged for a 100-percent loan makes the transaction fundamentally undoable if you are paying retail. If you are considering that option, check and double check the property analysis you will perform to ensure you are making a wise decision.

The bottom line is: the higher percentage of loan amount you borrow, the more you pay for the privilege of borrowing. There is a balancing act here and it will behoove you to learn everything you can about the pros and cons of all of the available financing options.

### *Reason #2*

If you over finance your property, you can't consistently enjoy positive cash flow. For the real estate investor, cash flow is the name of the game. If you compromise by thinking that you will have only an extra $200 to pay out of my pocket each month, you will soon be out of business. If you do that 10 times, you have to come up with $2,000 each month simply to say you're a real estate investor. How smart is that?

I received a call from a friend who has several properties with a negative cash flow. The payments are eating him alive. The call was a request that I take over his payments and he would deed me the house. I couldn't do it because the rent was several hundred dollars less than the payment and I couldn't see a quick exit strategy.

If you don't have positive cash flow (or equity), your options are limited. In addition, your dream of leaving your current job to become a full-time real estate investor is put on hold while you figure a way out of your mess. Those who have gotten themselves into this mess in the first place did so because they either didn't do the math, or didn't do the math correctly.

### *Reason #3*

If your property is over financed, you will have a difficult time getting rid of it if the need arises. My advice is to make sure you can dump the property easily before you close the purchase transaction.

I also received calls from two separate investors who had property they had to unload. Fortunately for them, they could do it. Their loan to value was about 80 percent with no cash out of pocket when they bought. Both investors sold to me.

As a result of more experience and networking structure, I was able to resell the two houses in less than 48 hours. This was possible in our slowing market because my sellers were into the property without being over financed. I was also able to give my buyers a great deal with great terms that promised positive cash flow.

If your exit strategy does not include a winning situation for your end buyer, you do not have an effective strategy. Use this as a general rule: every transaction has to be a win-win for both parties. If it is not, then you shouldn't buy it.

Financing has its place. I seldom use any of my own money to close a deal. When I do use my money, I know when I'm getting it back. I'm not suggesting that 100-percent financing is wrong for the real estate investor. I'm saying that 100-percent financing is wrong in most cases if you are paying retail.

Any time you find real estate in which to invest at 80 percent of value or less, by all means find a loan for the entire amount if your exit strategy fits the loan. You will have succeeded in creating wealth and probably positive cash flow. Whenever that is possible, take the leap forward. Financing can be a two-edged sword. Over finance and you can find yourself choking to death. Used properly, financing can create wealth to help you realize financial independence, plan for the future, and provide you with the ability to give generously to a worthy cause.

## What is Creating Wealth and What is Cash Flow?

Too often beginning real estate investors confuse cash flow with wealth building. It's true that cash flow is essential to filling your wealth bucket; however, you can be building wealth in other ways that do not necessarily rely on cash flow. An example of that would be a long-term rental property. If the rent you collect puts you in a positive cash flow situation (and that could mean only $25 a year), you are still building wealth.

Every rent payment that tenant makes, which you in turn apply to the mortgage on the property, is money that is building your wealth. As long as you keep that property properly maintained, and are careful about who you select as tenants for your long-term rental investments, you should also be experiencing appreciation on that property over time in addition to the equity you are gaining from paying down the mortgage against it.

Long-term rentals are just one possible real estate investment opportunity and the pros and cons of that option are worthy of having a book written specifically on that topic. Many have.

The common denominator between this wealth building scenario and others that I have already provided is that the end result is that you had a working strategy to buy, make money, then if you choose, to get out and take that money to invest in a bigger and better opportunity. "Cash flow" is a generic term that can be used differently depending on the context in which it is used. We are using the term cash flow to mean spendable dollars generated after expenses are paid. Cash flow is most commonly used in real estate investing to evaluate the performance of a particular project or your entire business as a whole.

Creating wealth or wealth building is the dollars that you have earned and can add to your asset portfolio in either dollars or capital. Each time that tenant makes a rent payment on that long-term rental, you have just earned more capital that you can leverage for spendable dollars or sell for spendable dollars. The amount of money in your checking account does not define your total net worth. If you are doing it right, however, you will have significant cash flow and continue building wealth through capital investments simultaneously.

# Chapter 4

## Types of Real Estate Investing
**Purchasing Rental Properties**

Like the example just used to define "creating wealth," purchasing rental properties offers many advantages for an investor. Here are a few:

1. The tenant rent payments pay down the mortgage and build your net worth.
2. The equity in that property becomes working capital that you can borrow against and use for financing other investment projects.
3. If you maintain the property, you should realize appreciation during the term of your ownership (assuming that is for a minimum of a few years and you reside in a healthy market).
4. Multiple tax breaks are available for landlords for interest, depreciation, insurance costs, travel costs, repair costs, and utilities.

Before you run out and buy your first property, it would be wise for you to do some research in your area regarding tenancy rates, average rents and days on the market for properties similar to the one you are considering, so if you want to exit you have an idea of how long it might take.

A general rule is that if interest rates are down most creditworthy people can afford a mortgage, thus they are homebuyers versus renters. As a result, the vast amount of the renter pool will be those who are not able to secure financing. Nothing is wrong with that. A lot of people find themselves in a financial pinch at least once in their life.

However, you should take appropriate measures regarding tenant rules and regulations so you have the option to evict if their term at your property is causing it to depreciate rather than appreciate. Make sure you reserve the right to stop in at least once a month with a 24-hour notice to perform a property inspection, and exercise that right. You owe it to yourself to protect your investment.

## Lease Option
The Rent-to-Own approach (sometimes referred to as Lease Purchase or simply Lease Option) to home ownership is a tool used by landlords use to realize positive cash flow as well as help reduce their tax liability. At the same time, an owner can help families realize their dream of home ownership. The Rent-to-Own approach can be a win-win situation for both parties to the transaction.

## Why would a property owner want to sell by Rent-to-Own?

Investment owners enter into a Rent-to-Own for several reasons. For the buyer, a Rent-to-Own option is a form of creative financing that could result in:

**1. Low move-in costs.** The move-in costs are lower for the potential buyer, usually requiring a security deposit, first months rent, and a small "down payment" (option consideration).
**2. Immediate possession of a home.** If the home is vacant, you can usually move in as soon as the credit check is complete and initial fees paid.
**3. Allows buyer to build a down payment.** The option consideration is used for the closing costs and down payment

when you purchase. A portion of the rent may go to purchase price, which helps save money.

**4. Allows Buyer to repair credit.** Time is a great healer of bad credit choices when you seek credit restoration help. If you have filed for bankruptcy or have judgments against you, a lease option allows time to administer first aid to credit.

**5. The home usually has a fixed price at the end of the lease.** Knowing what the costs will be when you exercise your option and complete the purchase of the home is important.

**6. Permits buyer to move up in neighborhood.** You can actually live in an upscale home at a price close to the cost of a less affluent neighborhood. The fact is, the higher the price, the lower the monthly costs in proportion to the value of the home.

**7. Appreciation of the home while you are a "tenant."** You can actually earn equity in the home you are leasing. If the real estate market is in decline, you can simply walk away without any legal repercussions. In a Rent-to-Own agreement (specifically the option portion), the only obligation is on the part of the landlord to complete the transaction.

Why pay $20,000 or $50,000 down on a property when you can control and use the property with just a few thousand dollars out of pocket that will be applied toward the purchase price when you purchase?

Making the choice of how you want to control property and create wealth can be a difficult decision. It is, however, one that has to be made at some point as you consider whether to rent or own property. In the market of 2007, now is a good time to enter into a Rent-to-Own property. If you are looking for a home and want to own one in the next year or two, why rent when Rent-to-Own has such a tremendous benefit for you?

One of the benefits of renting is that if you don't like your location you can easily move to another one once the lease has ended. There are also drawbacks to renting that lead many people to buy their own home. When you rent, you are paying to live in a space that will never be yours. And then there is the third option we just went over—Rent-to-Own.

Let's touch on all three options now because they are options that you will sometimes need to evaluate in your purchase decisions and they are always options that your buyers will need to evaluate when buying or renting from you.

Each option—buying, renting and lease option—have advantages and disadvantages. When you are deciding about a property purchase as either your residence or an investment, consider the good and bad of either choice. Ultimately, you must decide if the benefits of home buying versus renting or lease option outweigh the associated costs and benefits.

**Home Buying**

The true cost of home buying is more than the down payment and mortgage. Another consideration is private mortgage insurance (if your down payment was less than 20 percent of the home price), homeowner's insurance, property taxes, and maintenance. Those costs can increase your monthly payment by as much as 40 percent.

On the positive side, in buying the home, each payment you make on your mortgage brings you one-step closer to home ownership. As you pay on your mortgage, you increase the equity in your home. That equity can be beneficial if you want to sell your home or use it to borrow money.

It's a well-known fact that mortgage interest payments and some property taxes are tax deductible. For many, that is a good reason for home buying. Not only are you investing your money in a valuable asset, but also you get a break from the federal government for doing so.

Appreciation is another factor in home buying. That's where you realize profit simply by owning the property and allowing the economy to raise the value of the property. Sometimes that can be significant if you live in an area of rapid price upswing. If you own a property for 10 years, the value of that property will likely double.

When you buy real property, property maintenance becomes your responsibility. You will either have to maintain the home yourself or pay someone to do it. In either case, it is an additional concern and cost that you must take into account.

## Renting

In a rental, the landlord provides general maintenance of the property and fixes anything that breaks down. When renting, moving is easier for the tenant. Of course, this depends on the amount of belongings they have, but generally speaking, people who rent tend to have less "stuff" than people who own.

Extra fees are usually nonexistent. Although some landlords require that tenants have renter's insurance, premiums are generally much lower than homeowner's insurance. When you rent, all you have to worry about is the rent and utilities. But you also have to consider that rents go up. That means that tenants will likely be paying more rent year after year.

On the down side, you could rent a home for 30 years and not realize any appreciation or profit. If you had bought rather than rented, in 30 years you would have a sizable asset. I have one tenant who has rented from me for more than 15 years. He has paid for my property. The value of the property has gone from $25,000 to $250,000.

## Rent-to-Own or Lease Option

The third way you can control property is through a hybrid alternative. In the Lease Option you control the property for a specified period of time and perhaps even enjoy appreciation without be obligated to actually purchase the home. On a Lease Option, you make a down payment in the form of option consideration that is nonrefundable. The seller will often deduct an agreed-upon amount per month from your purchase price, and you, therefore, built a sort of equity even while renting.

You don't actually have equity, but if you close the purchase you have money built in that helps with the down payment and closing costs. I sometimes refer to this as a "forced savings program" because it forces the buyer/tenant to set aside money in the event he chooses to close the loan.

Remember to do the math and to take the numbers at face value. You don't want to gamble on investments that don't look good on paper, even if you think all it really needs is your magic touch. Too many options are available that are a sure solid investment. Move on to those.

**Lease Option as an Investment Strategy**

Speaking directly to the investment side of purchasing, I think the lease-option strategy may be a perfect real estate investment vehicle for new investors. No other approach offers the kind of return on investment when a person is just starting out and has limited funds and investment knowledge.

Through a lease-option strategy, a person with little or no money can control a property and enjoy appreciation while experiencing an up-front cash flow as well as a positive monthly cash flow. I've written and spoken about these three aspects on several occasions. Not only can you make money, you can do so without the headache of being a landlord if you have the right documents. I have several lease-options in force at this writing and never get a call from a buyer tenant. When I was a traditional landlord, I regularly received calls from tenants.

A lease-option is an investment strategy that consists of two parts. One part is a lease, the agreement to possess "equitable title," which essentially means you have the right to live in and use the property free from interference as long as you pay as agreed. The other part is an option to purchase the property. In an option, the tenant buyer has the right, but not an obligation, to purchase the property at a later date.

When I'm a lease-option seller, I always try to get at least $5,000 down in nonrefundable money called option consideration. That sum is applied to the purchase price if the tenant-buyer exercises his option and purchases the house after the lease expires. I also try to get at least $200 each month in monthly positive cash flow. That cash flow is spendable dollars after expenses.

I spent $1,200 to have my attorney draw up lease and option agreements that has essentially ended all middle-of-the-night repair calls. If you purchased on a lease-option with the right to sublet (also called a sandwich lease), you can have the same benefit. It seems that life is perfect when you have the right agreements in place, but be careful. While all of this might sound great, there is a downside. Things can go wrong, causing you to lose both sleep and money. You could lose the house you leased or optioned and you could get sued for not living up to your agreement with the tenant-buyer.

**How do you protect yourself from these possibilities?**

**1. Check the Title.** If you are buying by way of a lease option, be sure you do your due diligence. Have a preliminary title report done (in my hometown, it's called a lot book report if you just want to check the title). You may find that your seller doesn't own the property or that he has so many liens against the property that you will never be able to buy it. The money you spend here is money well spent. You can also do the research yourself if you have the time to go to the county recorder and go though documents.

**2. Check Credit.** If you are the seller, be sure to run a credit check on your tenant-buyer. If you are the buyer, run a credit check on the seller. You will be surprised what you will find. *Rule of thumb:* Know as much about the buyer or the seller as you can before you sign documents. It is said that knowledge is power. My advice: Be knowledgeable.

**3. Escrow.** If I'm a lease-option buyer, I want to open an escrow account. I will open it with several documents. I will include a completely filled out purchase agreement (as an exhibit) describing the terms of the purchase along with a one-page lease-option agreement. I have the seller sign a warranty deed to place in escrow.

If he is off sailing in the China Sea when I get ready to close the transaction, I won't have to find him. Also, sellers sometimes experience seller's remorse before your lease it up. A signed warranty deed will avoid this problem. In the event of a legal action or challenge, that paper work creates a paper trail that spells out the intent of the buyer and the seller when the transaction took place.

**4. Option Money.** I always get enough nonrefundable option consideration to cover costs if my tenant-buyer wants to cheat me out of money. So far, I've never lost any money nor had a house damaged by a buyer tenant.

The more money your tenant-buyer puts down, the safer you probably are. The approach I use to get plenty of money down is to constantly refer to the tenant-buyer as a buyer. I let him know that I'm not looking for a tenant, I want a buyer. That usually separates those who want to rent from those who want to buy. The buyer mentality is much better for you than that of a tenant. *Rule of thumb:* If you are buying on a lease-option, use as little of your own money as possible. If you are selling, ask for as much as you think you can get to protect yourself and create cash flow. I always start by asking for $5,000 cash, or cash and part trade.

**5. Lease-Option Agreement.** Use good, solid documents for your lease-option agreements. If I'm a lease option buyer I use a one-page Lease Option form. There are legal reasons for that: I do not want a document too specific if I am the buyer. If I am a lease-option seller, I use very detailed lease agreements and a separate detailed option agreement and I caution my protégés to not use generic forms from an office supply store or free downloadable forms off the Internet when they are the seller. Remember, the stronger and tighter the documents when you sell, the better. When you are the buyer, use a one-page document.

**6. Notice of Option.** If you are the buyer in a lease option transaction, record a Notice of Option (it may also be call a Memorandum of Option) with your county clerk. For a few dollars in recording fees, you can go on record that you have an interest in the property. If the seller tries to sell the house from under you, you can stop the proceeding with that document. If your Option Agreement and Notice of Option have the right wording, you can even stop your seller from borrowing more money on the property.

**7. Insurance.** If you are a lease-option buyer, have a letter prepared for the seller to sign that you can mail to his insurance agent that instructs him to include you as an additional insured "as your interest may appear." This may save you money in the event of a loss due to fire or liability claim. If you are the seller, advise your tenant-buyer in writing to obtain rental insurance to protect their personal property in the event of a loss. The steps outlined are not all-inclusive, but they will get you started down the path of self-protection. People who lose money in lease options are those who have failed to protect themselves by using the properly worded documents.

## Hybrid Consumer

The lease-option market is huge. We market to a hybrid customer—not a buyer and not a tenant. We look for someone who wants to buy a house but forced to rent for one reason or another. We are looking for the person who has a credit problem, for example, and who believes he can't qualify for a home loan.

An ever-increasing number of people have credit problems. I run ads that invite people to the web site, and the response is good. When close to completing new projects, my financial lending partner and I will hold Saturday seminars for people who want more information about buying through a lease-option. By the end of the meeting, we generally have a long list of qualified people who sign up to become a tenant-buyer.

**Risk versus Return on Investment**

If you think you'll have sleepless nights worrying about whether a house will be leased when it gets done, you should not buy an investment house. If you don't understand what is going on, you should not buy an investment of any kind. Again, real estate investing involves risk. However, after you look at the facts, the risks are minimal, and I believe they are less risky than anything else available when you consider the return on your cash investment.

If you invest $5,000, for example, and achieve a return of $30,000, what is your rate of return? You would earn a 100-percent return on your money if you realized a $10,000 profit. If you made $20,000, you would realize a 200-percent return. If you made $30,000, your return on investment would be 300 percent. I would put my money in the bank if I could earn 300 percent instead of the 2 percent I earn in a savings account today.

If you had a strategy to get your $5,000 returned, and you succeeded and made $30,000, your return on your investment would be infinite. For zero cash, you make $30,000. That is a good deal in anyone's book.

**Icing on the Cake**

I once offered an option for people who are new to real estate investing and feel they need a safety net and mentor. For those who have partnered with me (they serve as a financial partner by putting down a $5,000 deposit and securing the financing), I offered a guarantee. I personally returned the $5,000 deposit within 30 days of closing of the long-term loan. What that meant was that my partner had **no cash** in the project. I still take on partners, but I no longer use this strategy as outlined here. Now I simply offer to partner with them with no personal guarantee. I have discovered that it is much better when your partner has money in a project.

Also my staff and I have personally marketed the property and found a tenant-buyer, relieving the new investor of the job. They were learning from me and could then do it themselves the next time. In the unlikely event that the house sat empty for a month or two, I would pay half the monthly payment until it leased, further reducing risk and encouraging me to get the house lease-optioned. Would I offer this for my students if I weren't positive of the potential for return on investment?

## Assignment of Contracts and Bank Short Sales

You found a good real estate buy and have a motivated seller who wants out of his house yesterday. Mr. Seller agreed to your purchase offer of $275,000 for his home appraised at $350,000. That is a good deal for Mr. Seller because he purchased another home and the bank will take the house back if he can't unload it soon. Your plan is to flip the house. You are going to pick up a few dollars in the transaction and sell it to someone looking for a property to purchase wholesale. But how do you get paid for finding a buyer without seasoning the purchase (owning it for a specified period of time)?

Lenders and some title companies are really jumpy right now about such a transaction. A member of the investment club I lead introduced me to strategy called a Reverse Assignment.

Here is how it works:

*Step One:* You find a good deal and Mr. Seller agrees to the price and terms of your offer.

*Step Two:* You disclose to Mr. Seller that you are an investor and your plan is to find a buyer who will take over the contract and close the sale in escrow.

*Step Three:* "But," Mr. Seller objects, "How can you accomplish this task when I have been unable to do so?" "Because I'm a professional. This is what I do!" you explain. Mr. Seller gets the point and says, "Okay, let's do it." You add your fee (whatever that might be—$1,000, $5,000, etc.—don't get too greedy or you won't find a buyer) to the purchase price and Mr. Seller signs a promissory note that is *payable at closing* for that amount. Now your contract price is $280,000 ($275,000 plus your fee of $5,000).

*Step Four:* You find a buyer (Ms. Buyer). Ms. Buyer agrees to purchase the home for $280,000 by way of your Assignment of Contract and applies for a loan with her lender.

*Step Five:* Ms. Buyer and Mr. Seller go to the title company to sign the closing documents. Since you have presented to the title company the promissory note Mr. Seller signed, you will be paid through escrow when the new loan is funded. Is Ms. Buyer happy? Yes. She purchased a home worth $350,000 for $280,000 and in essence created $70,000 in equity. Is Mr. Seller happy? Yes. He has unloaded a tremendous weight off his shoulders and has rid himself of the alligator that was eating him alive. Are you happy? Definitely, *because you get paid!*

Notice that seven things were accomplished:
1. Mr. Seller got his price.
2. Ms. Buyer got a great deal.
3. The deal did not require seasoning.
4. The appraisal amount requested was the original contract amount.

5. There is no feeling from Ms. Buyer that you were ripping her off because you didn't have to ask her to write a check in the amount of $5,000 for the assignment, which could have resulted in her going directly to Mr. Seller to cut a deal.

6. You got paid.

7. You are free to look for another great deal so that you can create more positive cash flow that will enable you to give more to your favorite charity/cause, pay your monthly bills, or build up your retirement account—or all of the above.

## Tax Liens and Tax Deed Purchases

Tax deeds are sold in 35 states throughout the United States. Almost every state has a method in place for recouping back taxes from delinquent taxpayers. Bidding and buying tax liens and tax deeds at government sales can be quite profitable.

Every homeowner must pay some sort of real estate tax to the government. If a homeowner fails to pay the required taxes on the property, the county will offer the property up for sale at an auction to help generate the lost tax income. During a tax deed sale, the property is usually sold for the back tax amount plus any fees, interest charges, and court costs. Because property taxes are a small percentage of market value, investors purchasing a tax deed can acquire full property rights at a fraction of the market price.

By law, tax deed sales must be announced to the public and are usually sold to the highest bidder. The winning bidder purchases the deed to property and becomes the new owner—obtaining all rights to the property, clear of encumbrances such as any mortgages, liens, or deeds of trust.

The tax lien and tax deed processes may be distinguished by what is referred to as the bundle of rights sold to the purchaser. In states using a tax deed system, county governments will sell full ownership rights to the investor. As of 2007, 17 states authorize the sale of ownership rights to tax delinquent property through a tax deed sale. Conversely, in so-called tax lien states, county governments sell only *their* right to the tax lien or tax claim on the real property. A total of 18 states have authorized sales of a county tax lien position to the public. A property tax lien is secured to real property as a first priority claim. The end result is a highly secured investment that is typically appreciating and can also be sold for more than you paid.

As with any real estate investment, you should thoroughly research the property involved in the tax deed or lien sale before making any offer. Do your homework and bid smart. You should also view the property and research its value before you bid. Another important point is that you should clearly understand what ownership rights you are purchasing through this sale. Each state has slightly different procedures, and remembering that not every state offers the same type of sale is important.

To find the dates and times for these types of sales, contact the county office where you want to purchase a tax deed or lien and check the local area newspaper. Words of advice, however. Stay local until you completely understand the process and what you stand to gain and lose.

**Building a New Home for Lease or Sale**
If I am considering building a house as an investment, I want to begin by first asking if it is possible to create wealth by building a house. The second thing I want to know, and it's almost as important, is can I create wealth without using my cash reserves? If I conclude that, yes, it is possible, then I want to find out how it works. So, let's take a look.

The figures below are used for illustration purposes only. You may insert your local information in the place of my numbers. The equation will work for your geographical area.

Let's assume that you find a building lot for the sum of $100,000, and you have a builder under contract to build you a house for $124,000. It would look like this:
Building Lot: $100,000
Cost of House (total): $124,000
Total Cost: $224,000

You want the house and land to appraise at about $300,000. Do you know why? You want the construction loan to be about 80 percent or less of the appraised cost. That assumes you have a lender who will loan you 80 percent of appraised value—not 80 percent of cost. If your lender will not loan on the appraised value, find one who will.

There are at least two good reasons you want the 80-percent loan to appraised value. First, it's easier to get a construction loan and "take out" loan if the value is an 80/20 split. The lender will look at the 20-percent equity position and rightly believe their risk is less than a 100-percent loan to appraised value loan. In other words, if you have a 20-percent position, you are less likely to walk away and leave the lender to pick up the pieces.

Second, the day you sign the contract with the builder, you know that you have created wealth. In the example above, you created $60,000. If you build two of these houses in one year, you created $120,000. In essence, once you have a builder, floor plan, and lender, and you arranged the appraisal that makes the project work, you created $120,000 with a couple of phone calls.

It's also possible to add your closing costs to the construction loan, and enough money to pay the interest for 6 months during construction. That means little or no money out of your pocket while adding $74,000, or more, per project.

One valid question is: Don, have you ever done this? The answer is, yes. At this writing, I have under contract more than 137 houses where this principle is in play. The exciting thing is that you can do it, also.

**The Appraisal**
What happens if the appraisal comes back with a figure that is at the cost of building? This does happen occasionally and when it does, I pass on the project. However, if you perform your due diligence, you should know before you spend the money on an appraisal how the figures will work.

**Do an "Arms Length" Appraisal**
I call my mortgage broker and ask her to call the appraiser and ask for information. I do this to have an arm's length transaction so that no one can claim collusion between the appraiser and me. It also simplifies things for the appraisers to deal with just one person.

After you run the numbers you have to determine if the amount of wealth you can create is sufficient for you to go ahead. For me, personally, anything less than $25,000 to $30,000 is too risky. I have seen eager novices willing to jump at the chance of a $10,000 profit margin, not considering that if just one thing goes wrong, which is always a possibility, the additional costs exceed that amount.

As you can see, when using the new construction model wealth can be created without putting up a lot of your own money.

**Rehabilitate a Resale Home and Sell for Profit**
Flipping, the real estate investment vehicle in which you purchase a property below value and soon sell it for a profit is a very good way to generate positive cash flow. Flipping has become a big business. I encourage my protégées to buy and sell for a profit without getting into the rehabilitation business if their

goal is to be an investor. In some states, you cannot fix and flip unless you are a licensed contractor. In those states, you must generally attend courses, pass a test, and become a member in the state contractors association. The rules and regulations surrounding this topic vary from state to state. Many states, however, still do not require that you are a contractor to do the work yourself.

The biggest mistake that most "fix and flippers" make is that they estimate how much it would cost someone else to make the improvements that you could do for less and then add that amount to their purchase price and voila, that's the correct price for the house. Major mistake. Knowing how to correctly calculate margins and profits on a fix and flip property is the difference between success and failure.

Holding costs are probably the biggest culprit for eating away profit. Too often some very expensive costs associated with fix-and-flip projects are overlooked until its too late. For example, if it takes 60 to 90 days to do the fixit portion of a flip, then you incur 2 to 3 months in finance charges and holding costs. If it takes another 60 to 90 days to sell your project house once you complete the project, it you are now negative 5 to 6 months of holding costs.

Holding costs are loan payment, interest payment, taxes and insurance (and PMI insurance if that was needed). Before you make a fix-and-flip decision, call your lender and find out what it will cost you each month to carry the house while you're rehabilitating it. That calculation should include worst-case scenario rehabilitation time and days on the market. Deduct that total right off the top.

Wait, we're not done yet! Are you going to sell your completed project as a For Sale by Owner or are you going to list it with an agent? If you are going to list it with an agent, you should assume the average national commission rate of 6 percent.

Now, add the rest of the closing costs such as title insurance and transfer fees.

If you're going to attempt to sell your fix and flip as a For Sale by Owner then you need to put together your own marketing and advertising plan. Where are you going to print ads? How much are those ads going to cost? You can also typically assume that if you are not listing your property on the Multiple Listing Service (MLS) where it can be accessed by all Realtors®, then your days on the market are likely going to be a lot more than the listed average. Plan for that because it will add to your holding costs.

In a fix-and-flip project, you also need to plan for at least an extra 10 percent in rehabilitation costs than your original estimate included. You never know what you are going to uncover in a fix-and-flip property, so you need to plan for that.

Now, if you have appropriately considered finance and holding charges, closing costs, unexpected issues, and commissions or marketing costs, you are much closer to determining what you really need to sell your rehabilitated home to break even. That's right, what are you working for if you don't plan profit for yourself? As a general rule, assume that you need to net at least 10 percent of the total sell price of the home in order for it to make sense. So add that to the costs column and NOW you have your sell price.

Stop! Before you say "Ok, I'll just sell it for that much then." The market doesn't work that way. You should determine how much homes with similar square footage and of the same age and proximity have sold for in the last 6 months. A house is worth only what someone is willing to pay. The buyer determines the price—not the seller. If buyers aren't paying what you want, your efforts will be fruitless and costly.

Once you have done the research and determined the correct selling price range, attempt to price your fix and flip on the lower end of that range so you can keep the days on the market as low as possible. Remember, each month you sit on the property is another month of financing charges that were taken right of your profits. Holding out for best price is a fallacy that will come back to bite you every time.

Another obvious consideration for fix-and-flip projects is the skill and resources required to do the job. Some people really can do it all and know how to do electrical, plumbing, lay tile, and knock down walls or re-drywall.

Most however, do not. If you are one of those people you need to take a serious look at what you will be putting into the project in time and labor. If you are not, you must get accurate estimates from professionals to ensure the work is done correctly. It all comes back to being honest with yourself about what the project will cost. If it doesn't make sense on paper, don't massage the numbers until it does. If it doesn't make sense, move on and find a project that does.

One other thing to consider for a fix-and-flip project is that it takes a lot of *your* time. Even if you hire the skilled labor, you are still the general contractor and have a great amount of responsibility. Remember that there are only so many hours in a day. Ask yourself if there is something else you could be doing (flip for profit versus fix and flip) that will make you more money in a shorter amount of time.

I am not trying to discourage you from using the fix-and-flip approach to real estate investing. I merely want to make sure you are aware of the pitfalls for novices. Don't fall into these traps. If you do want to pursue such an option, by all means, do it. But do yourself a favor and start small and start smart.

Perhaps your first project should be one that requires little more than aesthetic changes. A lot of dated homes need a fresh coat of paint inside and out and new flooring throughout. Replace light fixtures as well as kitchen and bath countertops and you have yourself a fresh feeling home, ready to move into, and worth a great deal more in the buyer's eyes than it was when you bought it. You can keep your costs down, do most of the work yourself, and still learn the basics of how the fix-and-flip process works. Perhaps you'll only make a couple of thousand dollars on the first one, but at least you will have learned the basics without going backwards!

**Conclusion**

Fix and flip can be a very viable method of real estate investing. The trick to doing it correctly is doing the numbers correctly. You have to be extra cautious with your purchase decisions to ensure you have a solid home that will be worth the list price you will need to ask to make your desired profit. Do the research regarding average days on the market, fair market value, improvement estimates, holding costs, and sales and marketing costs before you make a purchase decision. Time is money. Each day you have possession of that property is another day of holding costs you incur and comes off your bottom line.

Buy smart, be honest with yourself about the numbers, and fix and flip as quickly as possible to achieve the highest possible profit. Start small so you can learn the ropes and build yourself a rotary card file of resources and skilled contacts. Make sure that every improvement is geared toward the largest possible audience (neutral colors, nothing too far out of the ordinary). For an extra special touch, stage the home (bring in furnishing) when you are finished. That will be your chance to show off your natural ability to decorate while putting money in your pocket.

**Building Your Resource Team**

I included a chart that illustrates what your team should look like. Don't fill these positions with just anyone. It is imperative that you accept nothing less than the best! You need team members who understand your long-term objectives, have resources of their own, and want to create a long-term relationship.

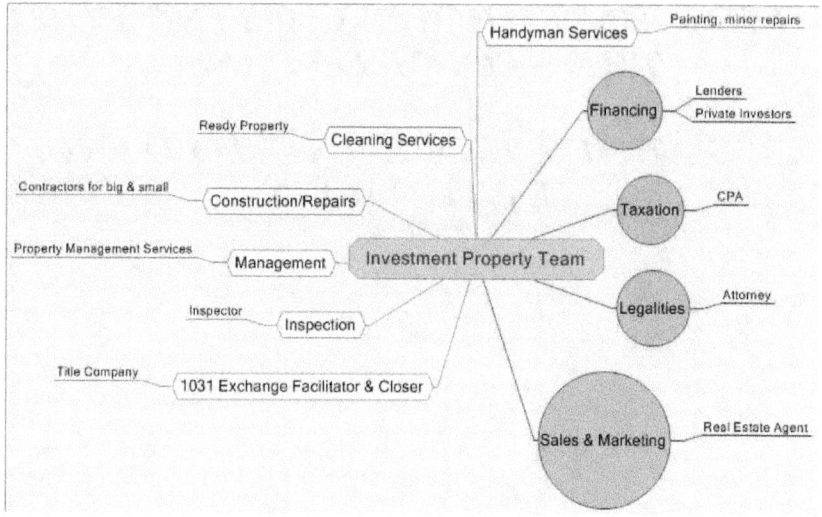

*LIFE ISN'T ABOUT WAITING FOR
THE STORM TO PASS –*

*IT'S ABOUT LEARNING TO DANCE
IN THE RAIN*

# Chapter 5

## Finding and Buying Your Target Properties
### Using a Realtor® or Go It Alone? Part 1

A Realtor® is a necessary team member for a real estate investor. A good Realtor® can assist you with research, locating good deals (expired and new listings) in a timely fashion, finding buyers or tenants, and a host of other services. In short, they can make you huge sums of money if you use them properly. The right real estate agent—or the wrong one—can have an impact on not only the outcome but also the entire process.

It may take some time to find a good Realtor®, but it will be time well spent. Ask other investors who they use. Later I will provide you with questions you should ask when hiring a Realtor®.

Some investors want to bypass the Realtor® because they don't want to pay their fee. I think that is a big mistake. The least expensive thing you can do in today's litigious culture is hire a good one. Why? It makes sense because a reputable Realtor® will carry an Errors and Omissions (E&O) insurance policy and is a member of an association that must adhere to a strict code of ethics. E&O insurance means you have recourse if your Realtor® makes an error in providing you with good information or proves to be incompetent.

Second, hiring a Realtor® means you are hiring a member of an association with a strict code of ethics. What that means is you can complain to the association if your Realtor® has done something unethical, or incorrect, and then seek mediation. Realtors® are experts in their fields just as accountants or attorneys are experts in theirs. A good Realtor® will have a strong network of connections you will be able to use to secure future transactions.

When seeking out a Realtor® for your team, you are not necessarily looking for the highest producer, or the one that has the most letters behind their name. Who you're looking for is the smartest Realtor®. You want a Realtor® who understands the process of analyzing a property and determining if it is a good investment or not before they call you. The right Realtor® can be one of your greatest assets.

When analyzing a property, build their commission into your costs so you can turn it over to them to sell and move on to the next gem waiting to be uncovered. If you use your Realtor® correctly, on both the buying side and the selling side, you can be twice as profitable as going it alone.

**Choices in Representation**
You have choices when it comes to real estate representation. The broker agent can represent the seller, buyer, or both. It's called the "law of agency." I suggest that you hire a real estate broker to represent only you when you are looking to purchase property. A buyer agency is when the Realtor® represents the interests of the buyer while the traditional model provides representation for the seller.

There are other forms of representations, such as multiple representation. It is sometimes possible that a buyer represented by an agent of your broker will become interested in a property wherein the seller is represented by a different agent of the same broker. That is referred to as a multiple representation relationship.

In a multiple representation relationship, the agents will continue to provide the services agreed to in the agency agreements entered into with each client. Agents will provide information and advice to all clients, but will not place the interest of any client ahead of the other. If clients did not permit this multiple representation relationship, sellers could be excluding some possible buyers from seeing their home and buyers could be limiting the homes that they may otherwise be shown.

## Dual agency (as provided by Wikipedia®):

The definition of a dual agency is one that occurs when the same brokerage represents both the seller and the buyer under written agreements. Individual state laws vary and interpret dual agency rather differently.

• If state law allows for the same agent to represent both the buyer and the seller in a single transaction, the brokerage/agent is typically considered to be a Dual Agent. Special laws/rules often apply to dual agents, especially in negotiating price.

• In some states (notably Maryland), Dual Agency can be practiced in situations where the same brokerage (but not agent) represent both the buyer and the seller. If one agent from the brokerage has a home listed and another agent from that brokerage has a buyer-brokerage agreement with a buyer who wishes to buy the listed property, Dual Agency occurs by allowing each agent to be designated as "intra-company" agent. Only the principal broker himself/herself is the Dual Agent.

• Some states do allow a broker and one agent to represent both sides of the transaction as dual agents. In those situations, conflict of interest is more likely to occur.

You will on occasion come across the special circumstances where multiple representation and dual agency come into play; however, the more typical scenario is that the buyer is represented by a Realtor® from Agency A and the seller is represented by a Realtor® from Agency B. What is important to remember is that you do not have representation as a buyer from your Realtor® unless a Buyer Agency contract is in place. If your Realtor® doesn't suggest it, you should. Just be sure to keep the limitations of the contract to a specific transaction (the best way to do that is use a specific address). If you leave the "what" part of what you are buying open-ended, the contract obligates you to buy all of your properties through them. As with any legal document, read it carefully first and understand your position before you sign it.

Wikipedia® has this to say about Buyer Agency:

**Buyer brokerage** (or Buyer Agency as it is also known) is the practice of real estate brokers (and their agents) representing a buyer in a real estate transaction. In most states, until the 1990s, buyers who worked with an agent of a real estate broker in finding a house were **customers** of the brokerage, since the broker represented only sellers. Today, if the buyer is working with a broker other than the brokerage, which "lists" the property, he may choose to enter into a buyer-brokerage agreement to be represented. (In some cases where dual agency is permitted by law, even the listing broker may represent the buyer). If the buyer does not enter into this agreement, he/she remains as a customer of the broker who is then the sub-agent of seller's broker.

Some real estate brokers choose to work only with buyers. The brokers are called Exclusive Buyer Brokers (or Agents). The National Association of Exclusive Buyer Agents (www.naeba.org) is an organization dedicated to representing buyers. There are numerous reasons to use a broker who specializes in Buyer Agency:

• Only an Exclusive Buyer Agent (often called an Exclusive Buyer's Broker and EBA) can guarantee to represent you in your home purchase.

• Only an Exclusive Buyer Agent can guarantee to negotiate on your behalf.

• An Exclusive Buyer Agent provides the true facts as to value, market/neighborhood conditions, and obvious physical defects.

• The high level of negotiation training and expertise of an Exclusive Buyer Agent levels the playing field when it is time to make an offer on a property.

• Because an Exclusive Buyer Agent only represents buyers and does not have in-house or company listings, a seller is always unaware of the price buyers are willing to spend during a negotiation, bringing the advantage back to the buyer and the buyer's wallet. For this reason alone, saving thousands of dollars during the critical negotiation process is quite common.

• An Exclusive Buyer Agent will insist that the buyer uses a qualified home inspector who will treat the buyer as their client, and not a customer.

• Listing agents (the ones with the sign in the front yard) and the company for which they work represent the seller, not the buyer. Their job is to get the seller the highest price and the best terms.

• The job of an Exclusive Buyer Agent is to get the buyer the lowest price on the best terms.

• Exclusive Buyer Agents will do a better job for transferees than for anyone else. They will give you the facts, good and bad.

• A listing agent cannot tell you about many things that would be detrimental for the buyer because they work for the seller.

• An Exclusive Buyer Agent will help you with your financing alternatives. They may advise you to be preapproved by a lender. Why? Because a fully approved loan makes you a cash buyer.

• Exclusive Buyer Agents have a legal and ethical obligation to put your interests first! It just makes sense. One of the most important things you can do when buying property is select the right Realtor® *before* you begin looking. The following are questions you should ask when interviewing Realtors®. The list comes from The National Association of Exclusive Buyer Agents:

• How long have you been representing buyers as a Buyer Agent?

• Do you, or the company you are with, take listings? Do you practice dual agency?

• What percentage of your personal business and what percentage of your company's business is representing buyers? Is the balance of that representing sellers?

• Will you try to sell me one of your listed properties before you show me listings from other real estate companies?

• Do you have information about For Sale by Owner properties?

• Do you have expertise in the purchase of investment properties?

• How many buyers have you successfully represented in the last 6 months? Can I have the names and phone numbers of three to six of your most recent buyer clients?

• What training have you taken that specifically relates to being a buyer's agent and representing buyers?

• Do you have any specific Buyer's Agent professional designations?

• Do you know the six fiduciary, client-level duties you would owe to me if I chose to hire you as my buyer's agent? (confidentiality, accountability; reasonable skill and care;

undivided loyalty; obedience to lawful instructions, full disclosure).

• What is your commission or do you have hourly rates or a set fee?

• Will there be a written contract?

• Do you have a list of home inspectors, insurance agents and reputable lenders for me to consider?

• What clauses will you incorporate in our offer, to protect us as buyers?

• How will you help me save money?

• Specifically, how will you protect my interests and why should I hire you rather than another agent?

Here are seven reasons why you should hire a Buyer's Broker:
1. Direct representation
2. Competent representation
3. Experienced representation
4. You need someone to be your advocate
5. You will make a better purchase
6. You have a written contract
7. The broker is accountable to you

Agent representation is just one of many legal areas that become convoluted with "if that" and "when they" scenarios that can change the dynamics is a split second. That is one other reason why it is important to find an intelligent Realtor® who understands your objectives and is willing to provide the time and energy to be an asset to you. Remember that this needs to be a two-way street. When you come across an opportunity that you can throw in your Realtors® direction, do it! Reciprocity will become a valuable key to your success with your selected Realtor®.

A Realtor® is one way of locating a "good deal" but if you really want to be successful in this business it is far from the only way. You are responsible for your own success and your own failure. If you are used to saying things such as, "I could have had this/that if only he/she wouldn't have . . . whatever, whatever," you need to take a really good look in the mirror before you dive into real estate investing. You will be your own boss, and you are your own worst enemy if you think that blaming others will provide you any form of security.

I'm often asked, *how do you find good deals*? I had a new protégé demand, "Why should I go out and look at the property? You're supposed to find me a good deal." She failed to understand that if I found a "good deal," I would buy it!

First, let's define what constitutes a "good deal." To you, that may seem obvious, but if you can't clearly define what it means to you, how do you know when you've found one? Consider the following factors when defining what a good deal means to you.

## What is your exit strategy?

One factor and perhaps the first to consider is your exit strategy. What are you going to do with a specific property? Is the strategy to hold, flip, lease option, wholesale, fix and flip, or?

Before I close a transaction, I know what I'm going to do with the property. Sometimes my strategy changes, but for the most part it pretty much remains the same. If I find a duplex in my home town that I can pick up for 60 percent of value I will clean it up, hold it long term (more than 12 months), and then sell it.

If the duplex happens to be in Klamath Falls, Oregon, which is about a 3-hour drive south from where I live, I will likely sell it with great owner terms for a small profit and move it quickly. I will take that approach because I don't want to manage property that far away.

## What are your goals?

Each of us has goals unique to us. I teach my protégés to write a life purpose statement and build goals around that. Once you understand your purpose, you are in a much better position to define your goals and develop a plan to achieve those goals.

If your goal is to create passive positive cash flow of $10,000 each month so you can live on $5,000 and give away $5,000 to philanthropic projects, then you need to manage your activity and focus on your objectives in a way that will enhance your ability to achieve the over all goal.

Let's suppose then, that an opportunity comes along that would take you in a different direction. Although it's a great opportunity, it might not be in your best interest if not aligned with your life purpose.

## What are your skills?

If you don't know the difference between a power drill and a chain saw, you had better stay away from houses and apartment units that need to be repaired before you rent them. Unless you are looking at a property with an eye toward learning something new, stay clear of properties that require skills you are unable or unwilling to provide. The investment opportunity may not be as good at it appears.

## What is your financial strength?

This one is a biggie. I've seen new real estate investors get deep into debt and unable to complete transactions because they tried to purchase a good deal, only to lose it and other property as well.

For example, unless you have deep pockets, you may want to stay away from vacant land. Investing in vacant land and building lots is a rich person's market—unless you are building houses as a strategy. There is generally no inward cash flow to help offset the flow of cash out. The good deal suddenly goes sour when you run out of money and lose all you invested in the good deal.

If you have limited resources, try to keep your investment purchases to single family homes at the lower end of the real estate investment spectrum—or a step above. Many more retail buyers and tenants are at this level, which means you have a greater chance of selling the house or filling a vacancy and ultimately realize a positive stream of income.

I know several people who got in trouble when they found a "great deal." They borrowed to the hilt and made payments on empty houses. That strategy will set you up for financial disaster. It matters little that you picked up a $900,000 house for $700,000 if you cannot find a buyer or make the payments for an extended period of time. The deal may be good for someone, but is it a good deal for you?

As you can see, the term good deal is relative. Lots of good deals may be out there, but be sure the deal is good for you. This segment is a reiteration, in a different way, of the segment that tells you that you have to run the numbers.

I've said it before and I'll say it again. If it doesn't make sense on paper, then it doesn't make sense. You are, after all, investing. Risk is involved; however, you can minimize that risk dramatically by asking the right questions, doing an analysis, and acting accordingly.

**Your Marketing Plan—Part 1**

One of the most important sections of your business plan is your marketing plan. This section is where you include a definitive description of your customers, market size, demographics, characteristics, growth prospects, trends, and sales potential.

The marketing plan is a document that outlines your strategies and describes how those strategies can directly influence the growth of your business. In the plan, you should also include plans for your future growth. A snapshot of a 3-to-5 year outcome demonstrates not only your commitment to your business but your ability to plan for the future.

A marketing plan outlines specific actions you intend to carry out necessary to attract the client or customer base that you will need to make your business successful. I once had a marketing professor who used the phrase, "You can't operate in a bubble and think you are going to be successful outside that bubble." Everything you present to the market "outside the bubble" needs to be captured in a comprehensive marketing plan. The marketing plan is the road map to the next phase of your business through captured clients and awareness of the services you are providing in your business.

Often you will find that marketing plans are a part of an overall business plan. In a real estate investment business where marketing your services to the general public may not be your first method of tapping into new business, the inclusion of the marketing plan into the business plan is still required. Going through the exercise of completing a plan is important and you should not only answer the questions necessary to complete it but ask yourself what the answers to the questions should be a year or two after you are out of the introductory phase of your business.

Tapping into the general public, versus just using networking, to secure future transactions is a viable method of achieving your goals. A marketing plan outlines the specific actions you intend to carry out to attract the attention of that future business. How would you do that?

If you include the marketing plan into your overall business plan as it is outlined in Chapter 2, don't just breeze over that section to fill the space. Give it some serious thought. Not only do you want to demonstrate to lenders that you have the ability to plan for future business, but you want to plant those strategies in the back of your mind so that if an opportunity that fits that strategy presents itself, you won't make the mistake of overlooking what could have been a milestone in the success of your business. Below is a very basic outline, however, it is a little more detailed than the one included in the business plan outline presented in Chapter 2.

If you are eager for customers to be contacting you instead of your having to find every one of them, you may want to give this some serious thought early on, not later. Remember, however, marketing costs money. I have seen new business owners go under because their marketing budget wasn't properly in line with their sales. Plan big, budget small, and be creative.

**Marketing Plan Research:** An overview of your market.
- What is the total size of your market or markets?
- What companies within your industry have succeeded and how?

**Customers:** Who are your customers?
- What are their values, attitudes, and beliefs?
- Are they local, regional, national, or international?
- Are they liberal or conservative?
- Are they rich or financially challenged?
- Can you envision your client?
- Will you target other consumers, other businesses or the government?

**Competition:** Who is your competition?
- Do your competitors have Web sites? If yes, list the domain names. Make a list of what you like and don't like about their sites.
- What are your competitor's strengths?
- What are your competitor's weaknesses?

**Your Company Strengths:** What gives you the confidence that you will succeed?
- What unique benefits does your product, service, or cause provide?
- How have you branded your company so you will be remembered? Think positioning slogans such as, "Let your fingers do the walking" or "Finger lickin' good." Are market indicators in your favor?
- Do you have a top-notch management team?
- Are market demographics definitely in your favor?

**Your Company Weaknesses**
- Are you underfinanced?
- Do you lack technological know-how?
- Can you find all the right people for the jobs if you are outrageously successful?
- Do you have an adequate facility?
- Do you have ready access to your goods supplies or suppliers?
- Do you foresee any intellectual property problems?

**Online Web site Promotion**
How do you plan to promote your site? Give a detailed listing of each effort along with its timeline.
- Are you going to use "pay per click" Search Engines?
- Are you going to hire a Search Engine Marketing company?
- Do you have an online public relations plan?

- Are you going to conduct an on-going linking effort?
- Do you plan to have weekly, bi-weekly, or monthly specials?
- Are you going to do anything promotional?
- Are you planning ongoing email campaigns?

## Off-line Promotions

- Newspaper, magazine, radio, or television advertising campaign?
- Public relations campaign?
- Catalog, brochure, or direct mailings?

## Budget

- Have you set a budget for your marketing?
- If yes, how far out did you plan the expenditures?
- How much will you outsource? If so, who will you use?
- How do you plan to generate the money to fuel your ongoing efforts?

## Profitable Prospecting

Prospecting will be your key to financial success. You will not be able to wake up one morning, declare yourself a real estate investor, clip your phone to your purse, and think that it will ring. Prospecting doesn't mean that you have to go knocking door to door as if you were selling cosmetics out of a briefcase.

Finding real estate investment properties can be done in many ways. That is the luxury of becoming a real estate investor, you have some freedom to work your own magic your own way, and sometimes without even getting out of your pajamas. I am not going to feed you some line about how you can get rich quick working from home and how the world is at your fingertips from your side of the computer. But, you will be able to find some opportunities online if you look in the right places.

We have established that using the Internet is one way of uncovering opportunities to explore. Let's go over some others: tell people about your new adventure. I have been in the real estate business a long time and it has been said that everyone knows someone who is about to make a real estate change. Tell people what kind of investments you are interested in and ask them to keep an eye out and an ear open for anything that fits the criteria. Tell them there is a Starbucks coffee in it for them if they send the information your way. When they do, be sure to follow through and send them a gift card to Starbucks for $5. It's the best $5 you will spend that week, because I assure you, another lead will follow shortly thereafter.

If you've been feeling a little cooped up but want to stick to your objectives, get in your car and drive around looking for For Sale by Owner signs. Not all For Sale by Owner properties keep ads in the paper regularly. They forget to renew with the paper or they don't want to continue to pay the costs for continued advertising. Take down the contact information on the sign and call them or even stop by if that's more your style. Find out what their objectives are and if they are willing to work with an investor to achieve their objectives in a timelier manner. Buy cheap, sell cheap, and profit.

Another possible source is identifying homes already vacant. Call them first (a normal source of information is the county clerk or a customer service representative at your favorite title company). It is pretty clear that they have already moved on and likely consider their old home a monkey on their back. Call them and find out what they would consider selling it for. Even if they're not ready to sell wholesale today, they might be ready after a few more double mortgage payments. Keep a watch for these properties and call them again in a few months if the sign is still there.

How about contacting landlords with For Rent ads in the paper. If the same ad has shown up week after week, then it's possible that the landlord is ready to call it quits. Of course, if the owner is unable to find a renter, perhaps there is good reason, and you will need to do a little research and figure out why before you write an offer. However, it might be something that you have the resources to deal with and still make a profit. Whichever it turns out to be, it is worth looking into.

Take this next suggestion seriously! Take lenders to lunch! Go through the yellow pages and make a list of lenders in your area. Lenders are a superb way of finding foreclosures before they are listed with agents or put up for auction. If you can put the deal together before they accrue additional costs, it may be savings they are willing to put in your pocket. Additionally, they are in touch with clients who have property they want or need to move.

While you're meeting with these lenders you can informally interview them and find out what their area of expertise is s well as evaluate if they are someone that could or should become a key player in your team of resources. Ask them if they know of any attorneys or accountants who specialize in real estate that would complement your team. You can also ask them about local appraisers and inspectors. Lenders are in a unique position because they come in contact with a variety of the levels of investing outlined in Chapter 2. Treat them to lunch and go prepared to do more than simply socialize.

Another great place to become familiar with is the courthouse. Many things such as evictions and foreclosures are required to be recorded with the county. When something is recorded with the county, it becomes public record. If it's public record, you can get to it. Take some time to visit your county courthouse and ask questions. Find out what is recorded and where and how you can get it. Find out how frequently it would be beneficial for you to stop and check for updates. Are they recorded weekly or monthly?

A fairly obvious suggestion is to put an ad in the paper. That ad should be very brief and should encourage anyone who would like to sell quickly, for any reason, to call you. Indicate that you are in the business of making real estate sales happen.

Government-owned real estate can be good bargains. Most investors have heard of Housing and Urban Development (HUD) homes and Veterans Affairs (VA) homes. Those homes are foreclosed homes that the government has taken back. They usually need a good cleaning, carpet, and paint. I know investors who buy only HUD homes and have done well. Many of these homes can be located on line. There is typically a little red tape involved to make offers on government-owned properties, but once you learn the process, it will forever be a valid way of uncovering opportunities.

If a large business recently closed or laid off workers in your area, there may be several families who were living pay check to pay check that need to unload their houses quickly to keep their credit ratings in tact or prevent foreclosure. This would be a great opportunity to work with these homeowners in a lease-option scenario. It will keep them in their house and protect their credit. You can purchase the house from them at mortgage value and sell it back to them when they get a new job. This same scenario can work with divorce or death situations as well.

Don't prey on the weak; rather give them an option to stay where they are, with their dignity in tact while paying you rent instead of the bank a mortgage payment and provide them the option to buy back in when they can. A good investor is always looking for the win-win!

## Don't Overlook the Details

You are a new real estate investor. You've found a good investment buy. What do you do? You make an offer to purchase. All states require that an offer to purchase real estate must be in writing to be enforceable. How do you do that?

The sales contract, sometimes called a purchase agreement, doesn't have to be a preprinted form or have any special look to it. It should, however, include several pieces of information that have an impact on the sale. Here are the key pieces of information that most sales contracts will include:

1. A legal and physical description of the property being purchased. The legal description is used by the county government to identify the property even if the street address changes. The legal description of the property will never change.

2. The selling price and method of payment should be included. In most cases, a mortgage or a note and trust deed is the method of payment. I advise you to include details about the amount of the down payment, loan, and earnest money deposit. If you have any contingencies regarding loan qualification for the loan, they should be listed as well.

3. If you are the buyer, you will want to name a title and escrow company that will hold your earnest money and close the transaction.

4. You should also include in your offer the proposed date of closing. If you think there is a possibility of not meeting that date, be sure to include a provision that states the closing date may be extended an additional number of days, if needed to complete the paper work. If you do this you'll not have to write an addendum later to extend the date and it may save the deal for you. For example, if you do not meet the closing date the seller can call off the sale. I've had this happen on a few occasions.

5. What's included and what's not included in the sale should be detailed. If the seller agrees to throw in appliances or a riding lawn mower (it never hurts to ask), those items must be listed in the sales contract. Otherwise, you could end up purchasing your own appliances after closing.

6. Any warranties included with the home should be detailed in the sales contract. A description of the warranty should also be listed.

7. If the property has a well and septic, be sure to define who will pay for the water purity testing, water flow test, and septic inspection and pumping.

8. A termite and pest inspection should be conducted. The sales contract should detail not only who will pay for the inspection, but also the party responsible for any repairs if infestation or damage is discovered.

9. The exact date that the buyer will take possession of the home should be included. That date can be anytime before, at, or after closing. I would include a provision that sets a set amount of rent the seller agrees to pay if he is not out of the house at the agreed date. I usually make the amount equal to my monthly payment.

10. The sales contract should include the amount of time that the seller has to respond to the offer, regardless of accepting or countering the offer. If you don't set a date of offer expiration, the seller could hold your offer for a month before responding. I usually give the seller 1 day to think over my offer.

11. Provision for arbitration or mediation is sometimes included. People do lie and deceive. And sometimes people are simply a big pain to deal with. If you include such a provision, you will likely avoid civil court action. The provision could save you thousands of dollars.

12. Either the seller or the buyer will have to pay for property insurance until the closing date. The sales contract should stipulate the responsible party.

13. Any property disclosures pertaining to the house should also be included in the sales contract. In Oregon, if the seller does not give you a property disclosure, you can withdraw your offer anytime up to, and including, the closing date. If you are the seller, be sure you give your buyer a property disclosure statement.

14. Any special provision should also be included.

15. If Mr. and Mrs. Smith are the sellers, be sure to have both sign the sales agreement. Here's a rule of thumb I use: It takes one to buy, but two to sell. You could get the closing with Mr. Smith's signature and Mrs. Smith decides she doesn't want to move. So now you're stuck. You can't take title unless both are willing to sell to you.

If I'm the buyer I want to have a purchase agreement with me when I look at a house. I may want to make an offer to purchase on that day. I may also submit the offer before I see the house. No rule exists indicating you must. Why not fax or e-mail the offer to the seller and wait to see if you have a transaction before you waste your time on a property you won't have under contract?

You can find forms you might need at Office Depot, Staples, or you can do a Google search and find online sources. Just be sure that your offer is clear and understandable and you have the seller in agreement with your offer.

# Chapter 6
## Doing a Buy/Sell Analysis
### Easy Math

Doing a buy/sell analysis for an investment property can be done many ways. If you spend some time researching the topic on the Internet, you will find hundreds and perhaps thousands of sites that offer software programs or kits for helping solve all of your problems and make the analysis as easy as pushing a button. First of all, do you really want the analysis to run itself with little input from you? As I have explained in different parts of this book, you are your own boss and you are responsible for your own success. It is important that you understand why you would decide to either purchase or not purchase a property.

You need to be able to see the bottom line as well as understand why the bottom line says what it says. The variables for making purchase decisions for various types of real estate investing tend to fluctuate. You must understand which variables are more important to what types of investing. Also important is that you understand the financial aspect of this business so you can gain financing.

Your lender will have a specific set of criteria required for funding. If the criteria are not met, he must go through his board or chain of command for approval. They will be even less responsive to a poor or high-risk financial analysis than the loan officer. If, however, one criterion for assessing risk is a little off, and you know why it is off, you can explain how your exit strategy for that property will make the factor a non-issue. If you can't explain the details of the financial side of the business, you will not be nearly as successful in the lending layer.

Let me tell you a secret. Lots of people hate math. The truth is you do not have to be an accountant to understand the basics of real estate investment analysis or lending criteria. But I won't lie to you either. You will save yourself many headaches in the long run if you take the time to learn some formulas frequently used in the real estate industry. Think of it as taking a nighttime cold medicine when you have a cold. It's horrible going down, but once you've made yourself do it, you are so thankful that you did because you will be able to rest so much easier.

As I mentioned, you will come across multiple analysis methods for real estate investment in your future research in this industry. I'll briefly describe for you the importance of specific areas in the spreadsheet.

The very first section captures the cost of the property, the down payment you must apply toward that amount, the interest rate, the term of the loan, and the purchase date. With this information included, you can calculate your principal and interest payment (commonly known as P&I). Obviously, the P&I payments are just one element of your monthly expenses but should be considered first and forefront.

The next two sections of the spreadsheet are about calculating depreciation deductions you can take because you own this rental property. Depreciation is one of the perks of being a real estate investor—ultimately putting more cash in your pocket. Using Uncle Sam's math, the deductions are valid and legal, which you can subtract directly from your gross income on the property, balancing the playing field a little.

Your income from the investment is coming from the rent you receive (in this long-term holding strategy analysis). It is always a good idea to investigate and find out vacancy rates in your local area and include an impact. If you plan for that up front, then you will help you be financially prepared.

The annual operating expenses portion of this spreadsheet is straightforward, and the purpose of this section is to remind you that you need to consider each category in relationship to your annual expense before proceeding. If you're simply "running some figures in your head," you might forget something that will come out of your pocket later. Use the spreadsheet and do the analysis.

If you fill in the information up to that point correctly, you can set up a spreadsheet like Figure 3 to populate the balance of the information. But, before you do that, be sure you understand what exactly you are populating when you will in the fields.

Your **Gross Operating Income** is your total income before expenses. It's usually a healthy number, and you will often hear investors who are "talking big" around one another throw those numbers around. Understand right now that those numbers mean nothing about the success of your business.

**Operating Expenses** in the analysis section of the spreadsheet is a reflection of the sum total of those specifics I encouraged you to review and accurately itemize. Those costs are the costs of holding the property with the exception of your principal and interest payment.

That calculation will lead you to your **Net Operating Income**. What you see here, if you're following along with the spreadsheet, is that although the terms sound fancy, they are really very simple math. It's more a matter of memorizing what formula each one means than being able to run algebra in your head.

The next step captures the reduction of your loan payment, which encompasses P&I payments. Once you deduct that additional expense, you have what is called

*Cash Flow Before Tax*. This number is a very important number. If it is negative you need to turn and walk away now. If it is positive even a little, you're making an investment that will earn you money.

The next step in this spreadsheet points out that P&I is not all money in your pocket. The only money in your pocket from P&I payments (your monthly mortgage payment) is the principal reduction part, much like the mortgage on your own home. Bear in mind that the real investment in rental property is the principal reduction you are gaining by using tenant rents to pay that mortgage. They are buying the property for you. If you keep that property in fair and working condition and do necessary improvements, that benefit of your investment will continue to be the strongest return on your invested dollar.

If you bring the Net Operating Expense that you calculated in part one of the analysis section, subtract interest (which is deductible), and subtract depreciation (which is also deductible), you then have your taxable income. Multiply that by your tax bracket and the total will be the amount of money that you have to pay Uncle Sam or that you saved yourself by properly using the deductions that are available to you as a landlord.

You will also see that appreciation can be considered and calculated into this analysis to give you a return on your investment (ROI) percentage with appreciation. My advice is that in a long-term rental analysis, always assume the worst—that it will never appreciate. If you do take care of it, it likely will appreciate, which can have a dramatic impact on the return on your investment. But, be level headed and assume a worse case scenario for your risk protection. If it never appreciates, and the return on your investment without appreciation is say....more than 10 percent, is that a good return on investment?

That question is for you to answer. If you have money in a 401K and you are averaging a 7-to-8 percent return then yes, it's not too bad. If you have money in a savings account earning 2 percent, it's great. If you have another investment opportunity where you can earn a greater return in shorter time with those same dollars, then no, it's not a good investment.

Even the very best analysis, whether the basic spreadsheet like this, or some complicated software sold through a convention speaker who charges thousands of dollars to come through the door, the bottom line is the same. You need to understand the formulas and the reason each of those formulas reaches the number that it does. You don't need to know how to actually calculate a specific set of numbers in your head; you simply need to know what the formulas mean, and more importantly, what those numbers mean to you specifically.

In my opinion, the most important formulas for you to concentrate on are the ones that bring you to your return on investment percentages. They are an easy way of measuring your time and energy versus profit. If your individual retirement account (IRA) is earning you 12 percent all day, every day, and you don't have to lift a finger, then you need to find "deals" that earn you more than that—or you are better off investing more money in your IRA than in your investment business. That seems like a very simple analogy, and it is. The truth is that if you did 12 deals in 1 week with a 10-percent return, then you are still doing something right. But in the beginning, think of the process at a basic level, and it will minimize your risks and improve your chances for long-term success.

As strongly as I feel about return on investment, lenders often refer to multiple other formulas on a regular basis, many of which take priority, in their opinion over return on investment.

For that reason, and to broaden your insight to the various methods of measuring the risk of an investment, learning some of the formulas is important. Use them on fictitious examples until you understand how one can impact another and what variable in the total equation that impacts the outcome of that formula.

According to Frank Gallinelli, the author of *What Every Real Estate Investor Needs to Know About Cash Flow . . . and 36 Other Key Financial Measures*, there are 37 financial measurements to consider. I believe this is a great book and one you should add to your library as a reference guide, but I am not advocating that you memorize the 37 formulas. I will focus on the most important (most common).

## The Closest Thing to a Crystal Ball

So far I have covered a few very important financial measurements in the spreadsheet and will touch on them again to help bring the picture together.

*Gross Income* is total dollars earned. In this example it is the rent that you collect.

*Net Operating Income* is the total dollars earned after expenses with the exception of financing and taxes.

*Cash Flow* is total earnings after subtracting all expenses plus finance charges (mortgage P&I payment). It is the total dollars in minus the total dollars out before the calculation of income tax.

*Taxable Income* is the income on which you must pay taxes. It is cash flow minus your deductions, such as depreciation and interest.

*Capitalization Rate* (Cap Rate) is the rate at which you discount future income to determine its present value. Knowing what the cap rates are for your particular type of property in your geographic area is important. Your commercial lender can provide you with that number. The Web site, www.realtyrates.com, can also provide that information.

The formula for cap rate is Net Operating Income divided by Purchase Cost. You can use this formula in three ways using those three variables. If you know the Net Operating Cost and have a target cap rate then you can calculate Purchase Cost. If you have the cap rate and purchase cost but do not know the Net Operating Income, you can calculate that. Banks and lenders throw the cap rate term around regularly. So take the time to really understand this formula.

*Cash on Cash* is another bank and lender favorite. The easiest explanation for cash on cash is the rate of return you receive on the dollars invested (your down payment) in any one given year. The calculation is cash flow before tax divided by cash invested, and it is a percentage. That formula is a measurement for evaluating how much you are making on the dollars you had to contribute to evaluate if they are in the best place. Could they be making more somewhere else?

*Gross Multiplier* is a measurement that does not take all variables into consideration. The figure ignores the time value of money and ignores the total operating costs, so it should never be used as a single indicator for purchase. The Gross Multiplier is the List Price (asking price) divided by the gross operating income (the total of all rent collected annually). Because list price is very market driven, so is the Gross Multiplier. If the Gross Multiplier is too high then the price is too high. For basic consideration, 4 is too low and 10 is too high. Do a couple of these on properties you know are good investments to establish a basic range for your geographic area. Because this is an easy math equation, you may find yourself doing this one "on the spot," which is fine, but remember it does not capture everything. You can use it to quickly determine if you will not be proceeding without further analysis. If the Gross Multiplier is out of whack, your final analysis will only prove it to be worse, not better.

*Return on Investment (ROI) or Return on Equity (ROE)* is your income after taxes divided by cash invested (your down payment). It is a method of evaluating if you are earning a great enough return on your dollars invested in this project. If you could be earning more somewhere else, you need to consider getting out.

The measurements I just discussed are the most important financial measurements. Not only because they are the most widely referred to but also because if used together, they provide a comprehensive evaluation of whether or not to proceed with this investment property. Of course, no calculator, spreadsheet, or software program can capture the variables that only you are capable of capturing, such as condition, location, and current market conditions. If all of those numbers come out perfectly but a new highway is planned to go through the back yard, the numbers are meaningless.

If you master these measurements before you make your first purchase, you will be more educated than a lot of "real estate investors". Don't be one of those investors. Set yourself apart from the crowd before you even start.

Recognize that if you want to do this right and if you want to be successful, you are going to need to commit to educate yourself, to some degree, in all of the layers of real estate investing. Again, no one is suggesting that you learn how the microwave actually works, but if you don't know how to use all of the features then you are likely wasting a lot of time.

# Chapter 7

## Use a Realtor® or Go It Alone? Part 2
### Selling Your Investment Property

One of the most challenging aspects of selling your house without using a Realtor® is putting the correct price on the house. If a house is overpriced, even by a few thousand dollars, the house may sit on the property for a long time. Some new investors think, "I can always come down in price, so I will price it high so I'll have negotiating room." That approach, while often used, is not well founded.

When your "For Sale by Owner" home has been sitting on the market for months without a satisfactory offer, one of the first things you wonder is if your price is too high. It may very well be. The house is not actually worth what the lender appraises. Nor is it worth the list price of the house across the street. It is worth only what someone is willing to pay.

Realtors® make it their career to understand the concepts of buying and selling homes. Selling a home requires an in-depth marketing plan that should include various forms of print, Internet, and even other forms of media advertising. Agents know when to hold open houses, how to price a, when to reduce it, and when to reduce it again, if necessary.

### Look at the Facts

Having made those statements, here is what I want you to do: Think about how many qualified buyers you have shown your house to. How many of them have made offers on your home? If buyers have been coming to showings but have not been making offers, or if no one is coming to your open house presentations, the problem could very well be that your home is overpriced. It may also be that a potential buyer has some specific objection. However, because they are working directly with the seller— you—they do not want to voice that objection. If potential buyers do not voice that objection, then you cannot address the objection.

Realtors® are middlemen for a reason. Their feelings don't get hurt when somebody says they don't like this or that. They collect the information and present it to a seller. Sometimes, if the seller addresses all of their objections, they may have a buyer willing to write an offer. The longer your house stays on the market, the less attractive it will be to buyers. Suspicion arises when a home has been on the market for more than a couple of months, even if the price is the only thing wrong.

But there is another important consideration. Others will use your overpriced house against you to sell their house. They will do it like this: "The investor down the street is asking $275,000 for that house. I have the same size house with a larger lot and I'm only asking $260,000. Mr. Buyer, you will save $15,000 and have a larger yard—if you buy mine."

A good Realtor® already knows all of this. They live and breathe it every day. They make the right decisions so you are not put into compromising situations. They know the pulse of the market, the average days on the market, who and where the competition is, and they network with the several hundred (or thousands) of other Realtors® in the city.

It is fallacy that you can save money by not using a Realtor®. If you take into consideration the advertising costs, the time for open houses, the time for all of the showings, and the time it took to put all of the sales materials together, you will realize they are actually underpaid by the time they split it with the other agent and their broker.

In addition to that, how much are you worth an hour? If you can make $10,000 a month flipping properties with the help of a Realtor® but only $5,000 a month flipping properties without the help of a Realtor® because you are spending so much time behind the desk or in your car running to showings, then the solution is clear.

As I explained previously, there are several layers to real estate investing, and you are not going to be able to do all of them yourself. You shouldn't even try because you will fail, and then your business will fail for the wrong reasons. Delegate anything and everything that you can as long as you have competent people to delegate to and you continue to keep your finger on the pulse of the macro picture.

The best part about Realtors® is they don't get paid until you get paid. If you see an attorney or an accountant, the clock starts ticking the minute you walk into their office. With the Realtor® you pay nothing until the time of sale. Why on earth wouldn't you take advantage of that?

**Do Some Research**

Even when you do delegate the sales aspect of your investment properties to a Realtor®, you are still going to want to understand the language that they speak and to know enough to ask the right questions. Pay attention to what's going on in the real estate market around you. Are there more listings in your area than there were last year?

If so, you will have to be a little more competitive in pricing your home. Take some time to visit open houses of similar homes for sale in your area. Compare them to yours. Take note of the negative and positive aspects and use them to gauge your home price. In the book *The Art of War* written by Sun Tzu, a Chinese General from the 14ᵗʰ century, he explains that if you want to succeed you always need to know your enemy better than they know yourself. That theory applies everywhere.

Look at your property and selling price objectively. If you were in the market to purchase a new home, would you pay your asking price? By asking yourself this question, you might easily come up with an answer about cutting your asking price. Don't let your sentiments or emotions cloud your judgment. Consider your home from the point of view of someone who has no emotional attachment to the home. This is a skill that requires practice but it is essential to being successful.

## Buyer Incentives

If you need to retain the asking price of your home, you might want to offer other incentives to get the attention of the buyer. Offer to pay part of the closing costs. Some lenders have a maximum amount that the seller is allowed to contribute. If your budget allows, max out your contribution to the closing costs. This will decrease the amount of cash the buyer has to spend and make the deal look more attractive.

Talk to your lender to see what can be done with incentives. Lender underwriting guidelines are always changing. Be creative and ask questions such as: How much of the down payment can I loan or gift to a buyer? Can I offer to make part of the buyer's payments for a few months? Be sure you have up-to-date information.

If after careful analysis you decide to reduce the price on your home, your Realtor® will advertise the new price. He or she will call any buyers that previously expressed an interest and let them know about the lower price. You might find that buyers are a little more eager to jump on the deal at the lowered price.

Pricing your house correctly could be the most important part of a successful sale. Rely on the expertise of your Realtor®

to provide the accurate information. Successful real estate investors have found that the correct pricing of their property is the key to real estate riches. Instead of pricing your house so that you have "dickering room," price it to sell so you can move on to the next project. Time is very important. Each day spent holding on to an overpriced house is a day lost in finding a new investment opportunity and incurred holding costs on the one you still have, and those holding costs are eating away your profits each day. Don't attempt to justify your reasons for holding on to the property.

If you are a real estate investor you will likely find yourself taking on the role of real estate agent on occasion. When you do, you must cover all bases adequately. To get top dollar for your property, your home should be in excellent condition and ready to be shown to potential buyers. Preparing the house to show is not difficult, but to ensure success it does require proper planning and a little bit of work on your part. If you aren't going to use the services of a Realtor®, then you had better be able to see through their eyes, and what that really means is seeing through the eyes of the buyer.

**Outside**
First impressions are lasting ones. The outside of your home is the first thing potential buyers will see so make it clean and attractive. "Curb appeal" is what attracts potential buyers. Spruce up the outside to lure potential buyers inside. In an established neighborhood, I try to offer a neatly manicured lawn. Manicured lawns implicitly signify a well-maintained home. Make a habit of cutting your lawn weekly while the home is for sale. Consider hiring a landscape service. You can save tremendous time and effort as well as keep it looking topnotch.

Be sure to rake leaves and to sweep the sidewalks on the weekends when your house is to be shown. If you have shrubs and trees, remove debris and dead limbs to make the yard more presentable. Planting extra flowers for color or setting out potted flowers also enhances a buyer's first impression of your home.

If there is a fence, make sure it is in good shape. Consider doing repair work, if necessary, and touch it up with stain or paint. Put away lawn equipment, children's toys, and any other outdoor items. Potential buyers want to see clean and green. If you have large pets, take them to the neighbors, if possible, so they don't interfere with the showing of your for property.

**Inside**

The inside of your home is next on the list. People generally buy homes that appear spacious, clean, and solid. Dark colors and clutter turn off most buyers. Store everything you can live without.

If you paint your interior, use an off-white or eggshell-colored paint. You should also replace your light bulbs with brighter, higher wattage bulbs. Again, the look you are going for is bright and spacious. Clean everything thoroughly, including having carpets shampooed.

Remove as many personal items as possible. The pictures on your refrigerator door are important to you—not your potential buyer. Buyers want to visualize *their* personal items in the house, not yours—so help them. Besides, the more personal items you remove or pack away, the more spacious and clean the home will look.

Clean the oven and all appliances and be sure to polish any chrome fixtures. Be especially particular about ridding your home of any odors. Fix loose doorknobs, repair broken windowpanes or leaky windowsills. Be sure all light fixtures are secure and in good repair. Also, be sure to repair leaky pipes and reapply caulk as needed. Consider hiring a cleaning service. They can make a remarkable difference in the overall appearance of your home.

## Home Inspection

Most people have a home inspection before they buy. You might want to head off a possible problem by hiring your own home inspector. He will give you a list of repairs that need to be made before selling the house. Use your judgment regarding his findings and repair anything that is a safety or functional issue.

Use the report to show potential buyers that you had the home inspected and you had the deficiencies repaired. Most buyers will accept your inspection report and not order their own. That fact is to your favor and may save you money in the long run.

The general tips I present here will get you started on preparing your home for showing. When finished, go through your home with an especially critical eye, trying to view the home from a buyer's perspective. It might also help to have a friend or neighbor to do a walk through of the home and critique your efforts. This will ensure a complete and thorough preparation that should boost the appeal of your home and make for a successful sale.

## Plan Your Work and Work Your Plan

Until recently, investors could purchase anything in my local market and be assured of a quick profit. They could make bad choices and still look good. Some of those same people are now feeling the pinch of reality as the local market slows to a more normal rate.

Having been in robust markets that have cooled to a recession level (a recession being when *they* lose money, a depression being when *I* do), I know professional real estate investors can do certain things to prosper in any market. Here are my steps:

## Have a Plan

The first step is to have a plan. If you don't have a plan, you are planning to fail—as the saying goes. Having a plan assumes you have clearly defined and written goals. If you work your plan on a daily basis you will create wealth as you achieve your goals. Included in your plan should be time for business, family, and spiritual—don't forget the spiritual part of the equation. It brings the whole into balance.

## Make a Schedule

The second step is working a schedule. If you want to prosper, make a schedule and keep to it. Plan your day. You want to control events rather than have them control you. Have a fixed time each day for prospecting when you do not take phone calls, a time for appointments, and to going to real estate closings. You will create more wealth if you discipline yourself to follow this simple second step.

## Prioritize Your Activity

The third step is prioritizing. Not all activity on your schedule is of the same importance. Do the most important things first and work down your list. If you have to find the funds to close a transaction, keep at it until you have it done. Tasks that have less importance can be relegated to an assistant. My assistant relives me of a great deal of work.

## Work Only With Motivated Sellers and Qualified Buyers

The fourth step is spending time talking only to motivated sellers and qualifying your prospects. Talking to sellers who are not motivated is a waste of time. In the inflated equity of our local market, many people have put their houses up for sale just to see what will happen and hoping to get lucky. If a seller is not motivated the results can be discouraging and a waste or your time.

Don't waste the buyer's time either. You can easily determine if a buyer is serious or simply dreaming. They can dream on your time as long as you are secure knowing that you can help them achieve the dream, and you aren't investing too many hours on their dreams and too few on your own.

## Education

The fifth step is taking time each day to further your education. Learn different techniques that will make you a better buyer, seller, negotiator, entrepreneur, closer, or keep you current with markets and trends. I spend the first hour of each morning increasing my real estate knowledge. At the gym each morning, you will find me reading a book on an investment-related subject while doing my cardio.

## Attitude

The sixth step involves having the right kind of attitude. The fact is that bad things can happen during the day. The question becomes, will it control you or will you deal with the bad stuff and make something good out of it?

All of us face circumstances we did not plan. What helps make one person successful is how he or she handles the unexpected. I embrace the philosophy that says there is good in all situations—you just have to look for it. If a deal turns into a lemon, I try to make lemonade with it, sell it, and create wealth.

## Plan to Give

The seventh step involves an idea that has been relegated to the rear of the philosophical bus. Most books and articles that tell us how to be successful are focused on "me." They are all about what *I* want, when *I* want it. I think that is dead wrong. If you want to truly enjoy success, you must first learn how to give away your wealth to others.

The principle of reciprocity is very real. The more you give, the more you get. I suggest that you learn to give away at least 10 percent of whatever you earn. If you cannot do that, your wealth owns you rather than you owning it. You can give to a charitable cause (you may even want to start one), educational foundations, mission projects—the list is endless—just give it with the thought of not receiving anything in return.

The result will be a satisfying, rich life. I give to others to enrich their lives. I not only share my wealth but also my time. For example, on Fridays I donate my time to an investment group with the goal of helping budding real estate investors. Learn to give, and you'll be amazed at the results.

You can survive and even thrive in a slowing market. You just have to work smarter and plan for your success. Follow the seven steps and you will do just fine in any market.

## Your Marketing Plan, Part 2

After you have secured a real estate investment you will, at some point, want to market that property. To reiterate, the obvious way to market is to hire a Realtor® who will do the work for you. In fact, there are several good reasons to do just that—especially if you are not ready for the emotional roller coaster ride of dealing with potential buyers. The broker fee, however, is money well spent.

However, let's assume again, that you want to try it on your own. Several options are available. This is the age of electronic information. Take advantage of the widespread use of the Internet to advertise your house. The Internet offers creative ways to help sell your home. Some are tried and true methods while others are a slightly more cutting edge.

## For Sale by Owner Web sites

One of the most popular ways that home sellers use the Internet is with For Sale by Owner Web sites. The Web sites allow you to list your home with pictures and a short description for a monthly fee. Some of the Web sites are www.forsalebyowner.com and www.fsbo.com. You can easily find additional Web sites by using an Internet search engine such as Google and Yahoo. The best way to find a Web site to list your property is peruse them individually for the cost and the features provided. You should also look at several sites before making a final decision.

The downside to using such a service is that you have to be available to answer questions. If you don't check your e-mail regularly and respond to inquiries promptly, the potential buyer will go elsewhere. Internet-savvy buyers have no patience. They want answers now. I have also found them to be shoppers who will waste much of your time.

Be prepared for disappointment. I've had a potential buyers sound interested and some have even wanted to make an offer over the phone without seeing the house. One couple wanted it so much that they verbally offered me $200,000 down on a $335,000 purchase with owner carry. I was elated. I even bragged on myself. My wife and I went out and had a celebration dinner. Unfortunately, I never heard from them again.

**Craigslist**
You can advertise your home for free on Craigslist.org, a free online classified Web site. Through Craigslist, you can place an advertisement for the sale of your house as a For Sale by Owner home. There are two major benefits of listing your home on this Web site. First, the listing is free. There are few, if any, other advertising methods that are free. The second benefit is that millions of people visit the Craigslist each day. You can even post pictures of your house to go with the text.

**Classified Ads**
Placing an online classified ad with your local newspaper is another option for advertising your house. The easiest way to find out if your local newspaper has a Web site is by using a search engine. The paper version of the newspaper might also make reference to its online counterpart. In some cases, the cost

of running a classified ad on the online version of the newspaper is the same as it would be with the newspaper.

My hometown paper, will place your ad online free of charge if you place the classified ad in the newspaper. I use this technique regularly with good success. I try to give only enough information for the potential buyer to call me. Some people will spend hundreds of dollars on a single classified ad, tell everything there is to tell about the house, and never have a call. If you give too much information you won't get any calls. Smaller ads are easier on your marketing budget, also.

**Develop a Web site**
Developing a Web site is easier than it has ever been before. You can easily obtain a domain name and a Web site to advertise on for a low monthly cost. Services such as www.web.com, www.register.com, and www.godaddy.com offer simple, low-cost options for setting up your domain name and Web site—even if you've never built a Web site before. Depending on the service you use, you might even find free templates for your Web site. You can use your street address or your phone number for a domain name and use it on your yard sign and marketing material driving people to your site.

Your own technical expertise can be a limiting factor with creating a Web site to showcase your home. If you are going to market your own property, educating yourself about current marketing trends is a good idea. You will be competing with experienced brokers. They have the advantage of knowing the marketing activities that start the phones ringing. You need that kind advantage, as well.

The benefit of creating your own Web site is that you can customize it to look the way you want it to. One major hindrance is that you must let people know the Web site is there for them to find. I place ads that have my Web site address instead of a phone number. One such Web site is www.YesShowMeHow.com. Take a look. People go to the Web site, read what I have to say, and then contact me by e-mail.

You can also do a Google ad, which will result in what is referred to as pay per clicks fee (each time someone clicks on your site, you are charged a few cents). I don't know of anyone who has taken this route in selling a specific property, but I might one day. I do run Google ads that drive viewers to my investment Web site when they search for specific words. You can get the information about Google ads by going to www.google.com and following the information.

**Finally . . .**

With so many options available to you through the Internet, you should choose at least one. So many homebuyers are using the Internet to purchase their homes that establishing your presence there is important. Now that you have decided to build or buy an investment house, what will you do with it? It's not enough just to have a house built. Remember, the goal is to create wealth. Before you build an investment house, have a plan in place. The plan can be as simple as building 1 house each year for 10 years and then retiring and living off the income produced by those 10 houses.

That is a simple plan but it works, as I learned from a mentor of mine named Barney Zick. In some of my investment meetings, I show my protégés how they can exercise that plan and retire with an approximate income of $100,000 a year for the rest of their lives.

My son has also developed a powerful and dynamic plan that we offer on our Web site. It shows how you can create more than $100,000 in less than 3 years using no cash out-of-pocket or credit. The plan can work even if you have the lowest credit scores possible—even if you filed for bankruptcy yesterday. The point is, have a plan.

We went over some marketing plan specifics in Chapter 5, in the segment entitled Your Marketing Plan, Part 1. I encourage you to review that chapter again after you complete this chapter. Both segments are intended to drive home the message that you have a responsibility to your own success. You can succeed if you take the right steps and perform the right actions. The information in this chapter is not intended to be redundant, but rather to repeat a very important aspect that may be the foundation of your success or failure.

**Why Have a Marketing Plan?**
1. You have a business that operates with purpose, not by accident.

2. Having a plan allows you set deadlines and hold yourself and others accountable so everything gets done.

3. A plan is a concrete result you put out for your mind to focus on and strive to achieve.

4. A plan helps you clarify what you want to accomplish in the next _____ days (you fill in blank).

5. You can identify the activity needed to achieve your plan.

6. A marketing plan allows you to think about your tasks and which ones that would be best outsourced.

7. A plan provides an opportunity for you to be free to concentrate on your highest payoff activity.

# Chapter 8

## Keeping Uncle Sam Out of Your Pocket Legally
### 1031 Exchange

The concept of 1031 Exchange or some counterpart of it has been available to investors since 1921, yet it remains the best-kept secret in the country. The opportunity to use the 1031 Exchange is nationwide. You can use it anywhere in the United States and for state-to-state transactions. 1031 Exchange is a great, legal way to keep your investment dollars in your pocket tax-free. If you are serious about real estate investing, then you need to be serious about learning the techniques to hold on to your money.

A 1031 Exchange is a transaction under U.S. law that specifies under section 1031 of the Internal Revenue Code, section 1031, title 26, United States Code, the following:

No gain or loss shall be recognized on the exchange of property held for productive use in a trade or business or for investment if such property is exchanged solely for property of like kind which is to be held either for productive use in a trade or business or for investment.

A 1031 Exchange allows taxpayers to defer capital gains taxes resulting from the sale of investment property, when they use a Qualified Intermediary, follow the Internal Revenue Service (IRS) guidelines, and use the proceeds of the sale to buy more investment property within 180 days of sale. To obtain full benefit, the replacement property must be of equal or greater value, with equal or greater debt, unless the taxpayer adds cash to the deal to replace debt instead, and all of the proceeds from the relinquished property must be used to acquire the replacement property.

The taxpayer must have assigned his interest in the relinquished property to a Qualified Intermediary before the close of the sale so the taxpayer loses control of the funds before he has any opportunity to obtain them.

At the close of the relinquished property sale, the proceeds are sent by the closing agent to the Qualified Intermediary, who holds the funds until such time as the transaction pertaining to the replacement property is ready to close. Then the proceeds from the sale of the relinquished property are deposited by the Qualified Intermediary to purchase the replacement property, which is then delivered to the taxpayer, all without the taxpayer ever having "constructive receipt" of the funds.

Additionally, the next property for purchase is required to be identified within 45 days of the sale of the first property and the transaction must be complete within 180 of the closing of the first property. Some required planning is involved before being able to exercise all of the benefits that are available with a 1031 Exchange. The deadlines are actually part of the Internal Revenue Code and cannot be extended for any reason except by a Presidential Disaster Declaration. The deadline is not even extended if it falls on a Saturday, Sunday, or legal holiday.

Don't let those requirements discourage you, however. The reality is, because you are required to use a Qualified Intermediary, they are the ones who need to understand and clearly advise you of how the process works. You will not be going through this alone with a blindfold on.

That said, it is also important to emphasize that the rules regarding identification are extremely important. Any attempt to backdate documents to make a transaction appear as though it is within the exchange identification or close period is against the law and considered fraud. There was a case that went to court in 1999 on that very topic, and the investor was charged almost $1.8 million in back taxes and fraud penalties. It is not worth losing your shirt over. If you are unable to put an investment transaction together within the IRS guidelines, then move on—skip it—and do it for the next property instead.

Some flexibility in the identity portion exists for this type of transaction. For example, if you haven't picked out which property you are going to be purchasing next, you can submit a list instead of a single address. You can also change that list anytime within the 45-day period using the appropriate amendment paperwork. The property must, however, be on the list.

The prevailing idea behind the 1031 Exchange is that because the taxpayer is merely exchanging one property for another property of "like-kind," the taxpayer receives nothing that can be used to pay taxes. All the gain is still locked up in real estate and so no gain or loss can be claimed.

An alternative for using the 1031 Exchange would be that each time you take a property into possession, then sell that property for greater than the loan amount, you would be required to pay capital gains taxes on that amount because it is considered income, even if you are putting those same dollars right back into the sale of another property.

I assume that you are wondering why 1031 Exchanges aren't very common if they are such a great thing. Well, the primary reason is likely that people do not know about it. People who understand 1031 Exchanges work use them routinely. A second reason may be that the conditions were not right for a 1031 Exchange. Some strict rules that apply to its use exist, and those rules are not flexible and not always logical.

A 1031 Exchange is intended to be used for investment properties purchased with the intent of being held as an investment property, not for a "flipper" or dealers and contractors who are in the business of buying and selling property. Of course, intent is hard to prove, and the law does not require that you hold a property for an exact number of days before you exchange it for another. However, if you're frequently exchanging properties in a short period of time, be prepared to explain to the IRS why you were doing that and, if audited, still applying the benefits of a 1031 Exchange.

A 1031 Exchange is also not designed for use on a personal residence. There are legal loopholes in the system that will allow you to convert your personal residence to an investment property before sale, but you should not move into the newly purchased exchange property. Remember, a 1031 Exchange is applicable if the intent is for investment property. So, if you move in within the first year or two, you are inviting an audit.

Vacation properties are a neat loophole in the 1031 Exchange rules. If you hold an investment property that happens to be a vacation residence, you are allowed to incorporate the benefits gained from doing a 1031 Exchange at the time of sale. To demonstrate the intent of investment, you must rent it during ownership. You can use it, but you must fulfill the investment obligations that are scrutinized in the process of a 1031 Exchange.

You can also rent an investment property to a family member as long as you still treat the investment property as an investment and charge fair market rent for it. Now that I've described in a little more detail where you might take advantage of 1031 Exchange and why you would want to, I will address the how part. This is the sequence of events that would take place if an investor elected to use a 1031 Exchange in the sale of her property:

1. An investor decides to sell investment property and do a 1031 Exchange. He contacts a Qualified Intermediary (QI), and they enter into an agreement.

2. The investment property is put on the market.

3. An offer to purchase the investment property is accepted and the QI signs.

4. Escrow for the sale is opened, and a preliminary title report produced.

5. The QI sends the required exchange documents to the escrow closer for signing at property closing.

6. Escrow closes.

7. Within the first 45 days after close of escrow on the sale of the relinquished property, the investor identifies replacement properties as required by law. This is known as the "Identification Period."

8. Within 180 days after the close of escrow on the sale of the relinquished property, the investor closes on one of the replacement properties ,which he has identified in that 45 day Identification Period. This is referred to as the "Exchange Period." The action completes the exchange. No cash is taken by the exchanger.

To qualify for this exchange, certain rules must be followed:

1. Both the relinquished property and the replacement property must be held either for investment or for productive use in a trade or business. A personal residence cannot be exchanged.

2. The asset must be of "like kind." Real property must be exchanged for real property, although a broad definition of real estate applies and includes land, commercial property, and residential property. Personal property must be exchanged for personal property. (There are some rules surrounding this—for example, livestock of opposite sex are not considered like kind property for the purpose of a 1031 Exchange.)

3. The proceeds of the sale must be invested in a like kind asset within 180 days of the sale. However, the property must have been identified within 45 days. Up to three properties may be identified.

Despite having learned a little bit about the when, where, and how of exchanges, you may feel as though some gray areas still exist in the execution of a 1031 Exchange. Let's go over the gray areas in a little more detail.

**Qualifying Properties and Like Kind Properties**
For real estate investors, qualifying and like kind properties are likely the most challenged as well as applied areas within the 1031 Exchange execution. As investors, we consider anywhere we put our money, assuming it is in real estate, a like kind investment. Perhaps different people or a different number of people live in them, but the intent is the same—to profit on real estate. I am sure it comes as no surprise that to Uncle Sam it's not quite as straightforward as that.

For the purpose of section 1031, a qualifying property is a property that is either used in a trade or business and held for investment. To qualify for an exchange, one must have a qualifying property, and that property must be put to qualifying use. However, understanding what qualifies the property and what does not is important.

In real estate language, there are two types of property—real and personal. Real property is land or structures affixed to land. Personal property is generally moveable, but real property is divided into three classifications: fee interest, leasehold interests, and easements. Fee interest is what is most typically acquired when one buys a piece of property. Leasehold interest is the right to use a property for a limited amount of time. It can be a few days or years. Leasehold interest property is not considered like kind to fee title property.

However, if the lease is a 30-plus year lease agreement, it can be exchanged for like kind fee interest property. Stipulations exist for 20- and 10-year lease arrangements that may allow those properties to be used in an exchange under specific contract conditions.

Exchanging a leasehold property for a leasehold property is possible if the properties have like lease arrangements. If you are going to be actively involved in a 1031 Exchange that involves leasehold property, I strongly advise you to contact your tax advisor for direction. An easement is the right to use someone else's property for a specific purpose. In some limited cases, easements may be exchanged.

Any property held for investment or used in a trade or business should qualify for 1031 Exchanges. Property that is not held for investment, but rather for personal use and enjoyment, do not, however, qualify. Property acquired for a quick resale does not meet the "held for investment" requirement and will not qualify.

IRS Reg 1.1031(a)-I(b) defines like kind as having "reference to the nature or character of the property and not to its grade or quality." The guidance states that "improved or unimproved is not material, for that fact relates only to the grade or quality of the property and not to its kind or class." An example of that includes an apartment building exchanged for vacant land and a rental house exchanged for an office building. The differences involve only grade or quality of the property, not its kind or class. They are all real property and classified as such, therefore, are like kind. It is also necessary that qualifying property be located in the United States.

You will hear some contradictory information on what qualifies as like kind. As already discussed, like kind is considered a gray area by most and therefore is open to interpretation. My rule of thumb is to understand the intent of the use of a 1031 Exchange. The intent is to move investment dollars in real estate over to a different piece of real estate that is also an investment. If you use real property class as a determining classification for like kind, you are within the scope of the definition the government provides and keeping to the intended use for which the Exchange was designed.

Let's discuss holding periods. Remember, qualifying property is property purchased with the intent to being held for investment purposes, or for use in a trade or business. The explanation is applicable to both properties being sold and purchased. Because there is no specified period of time defined in the tax laws of the section 1031 Exchange, such an explanation is another gray area. The investor must hold the property for a time period that demonstrates "investment intent." Because no specific rules exist in the law, I provide some guidelines that, if not considered, might land you on the audit list.

If you're going to hold a property for less than a year with intent to use 1031 Exchange, you are likely going to raise some questions with the IRS. There was a ruling in the past however, that a property held just days over 2 years was considered acceptable. Between 1 and 2 years, you are at risk for the exchange being disallowed and being penalized. I am not, however, saying that 2 years is the magic number.

Because intent is subjective, a reasonable argument for an investor is that they purchased the property as a rental investment, has not been able to find tenants, and is causing financial hardship. Another reasonable explanation is that the zoning recently changed in that area and the intent of purchase is not going to be granted for that property any longer. If that is the case, be prepared to show documentation regarding the intent for your investment property in relationship to any 1031 Exchange.

Remember, the burden of proof always lands on the shoulders of the taxpayer, not the IRS. My advice is play it safe until you have your feet wet and understand the process better. Generally, the investor must demonstrate their *intent* to hold the property for investment, income production and use in a business, or both. The longer you hold, treat, and report the property as investment property the easier to prove that holding the property for investment purposes was your intent. The shorter the time frame, the more aggressive and risky your position. Most tax advisors recommend that you hold title to both properties for at least 1 year and straddle 2 income tax years, but obviously the long the better.

I attended a seminar where an investor advised the entire class that if you put For Rent ads in the newspaper you will have proof adequately demonstrating that the intent was to hold it as a rental. The intent changed, however, after you were unable to find acceptable tenants (or any tenants). In my opinion, that is a bit risky, especially if you plan to use it more than once.

If I were the one doing the auditing, I would ask for copies of applications submitted, more than one ad to demonstrate you really advertised the property for a reasonable length, and ask for proof of vacancy rates in the area. It might work—once. It might even work twice if they are far enough apart, but I don't think you can use this tactic for each transaction if you are flipping 10 houses a year. I could be wrong, and you might be able to flip 50 properties a year using this tactic, but I sincerely doubt it.

## Examples of 1031 Exchanges

I've covered a significant amount of information in relationship to the 1031 Exchange. However, because of its uniqueness, you still might not have your arms completely around when to apply the benefits available through a 1031 Exchange. Here are some 1031 Exchange examples and what a real-life situation might look like.

Example 1: An owner of a residential home who lives in the country is transferred by his employer to another state. Rather than sell the home, which will no longer be his personal residence, he chooses to rent it for a period of time. After several years, he decides that he wants to sell it. At the same time, he has a grown son who will be going to college in another state. He decides that he wants to buy an apartment building in the college town for the son and other students to rent while they are in school. His house has appreciated from $200,000 to $300,000. Therefore, he arranges for an Internal Revenue Code 1031 Exchange and buys the new property, thus avoiding the capital gain at that time.

Example 2: A husband and wife bought a rental property before they had children with the intent of holding and renting the property until their children were through high school. They would then sell it and use the proceeds to pay for the college tuition for their children. Life doesn't turn out the way they planned. They have only one child, a boy, and he decides not to attend college. They have owned the property for 20 years and the property is paid for.

However, the couple has not done any updates and it needs attention. The couple feels they are outside their capabilities and just want to sell. Instead of simply selling outright, they elect to use the 1031 Exchange and select a piece of property they think might become prime property for a residential subdivision. They sell the long-term rental and buy the land. They have moved their investment dollars and avoided (or deferred) capital gains taxes.

**Different Types of 1031 Exchange Structures Simultaneous (Concurrent) Exchange:** The exchange (disposition) of the relinquished property (sale property) and the purchase of the like kind replacement property occurs at the same time.

**Forward (Delayed) Exchange:** A forward or delayed exchange is the most common structure or form for most transactions involving a 1031 Exchange. A Forward Exchange takes place when a time delay occurs between the transfer (conveyance) of the relinquished property (sale property) and the purchase of the like kind replacement property. A Forward (Delayed) Exchange is subject to specific time limits, which are set forth in section 1.1031 of the Department of the Treasury Regulations.

**Reverse Exchange:** A transactional structure is one in which the like kind replacement property is purchased first—before transferring (conveying or selling) the relinquished property to the actual buyer. The IRS provides guidelines, commonly referred to as safe harbors, for structuring reverse 1031 Exchange transactions, which the Revenue Procedure 2000-37 outlines. That guidance went into effect on September 15, 2000.

Reverse 1031 Exchange transactions structured according to Revenue Procedure 2000-37 are considered safe-harbor reverse 1031 Exchange transactions and those structured outside of the Revenue Procedure are considered non-safe harbor reverse 1031 Exchange transactions. Those transactions should be completed only with competent legal counsel. Reverse 1031 Exchanges are also referred to as both parking transactions or parking arrangements. If you are going to be involved in a reverse 1031 Exchange, seek legal counsel.

**Build-to-Suit (Improvement or Construction) Exchange:** The Build-to-Suit Exchange is a technique that allows the taxpayer to build on, or make improvements to, the like kind replacement property, using the exchange proceeds before they actually take title to the property.

**Qualified Intermediary (Accommodator):** If the Investor has the ability to access, control, or receive, or could have received, the sale proceeds after disposition of relinquished property (constructive receipt and/or actual receipt), the IRS will disqualify a 1031 Exchange, characterize it as a taxable sale, and subsequently assess the depreciation recapture and capital gain income tax liabilities. Section 1.1031 of the Department of the Treasury Regulations specifically requires a Qualified Intermediary, also known in the real estate industry as a 1031 Exchange Accommodator or 1031 Exchange Facilitator.

The Qualified Intermediary is assigned to the transaction on behalf of the investor as the seller or buyer, depending on which side of the transaction you are and hold the net sales proceeds from the sale of the relinquished property until the like kind replacement property transaction is ready to close. The Department of the Treasury Regulations provides certain safe harbor provisions when the investor retains and uses a Qualified Intermediary.

The Qualified Intermediary must be an independent entity who is not the investor, an agent of the investor, or a related party to the investor and who enters into a written like kind exchange agreement, qualified Escrow account agreement and the assignment, acceptance, notice and direction to convey documents. These tax-deferred, likekind exchange agreements must limit and restrict the investor's rights to the 1031 Exchange funds from the sale of the relinquished property. The agreement directs that the Qualified Intermediary acquire the relinquished property from the investor, transfer directly to the buyer, acquire the replacement property from the seller, and then transfer directly to the investor.

Several agencies provide Qualified Intermediary services. Some are companies that do nothing other than service buyers or sellers in their 1031 Exchange sales and purchases, and others provide the service with other real estate services. The price you pay for service can vary. In the past, I have used one of the title companies in my "team of resources" with great success. They charged a few hundred dollars for their services and that was it.

When you are looking for title or escrow companies for your preferred team of resources, ask if they facilitate 1031 Exchanges and how many they have processed in the last year. Also ask if they have an attorney on staff. You may find that if they do, you are receiving an extra layer of protection without having to pay for it. Generally speaking, however, the fees to complete a 1031 Exchange vary depending on whether you are completing a Forward, or regular, 1031 Exchange; a Reverse 1031 Exchange; an Improvement (build-to-suit or construction) 1031 Exchange; or a Personal Property 1031 Exchange. Before proceeding with a facilitator, ask to see a copy of the documentation so you know that they know how to proceed—regardless of type.

There is no limit as to how many properties you can have within the same 1031 Exchange transaction. However, practical issues should be considered. You may have more flexibility in these situations by structuring each relinquished property in a separate transaction. Talk with your attorney and your 1031 facilitator.

### If You Want the Cash
You do not have to reinvest 100 percent of the net sales proceeds from the sale of one of your investment properties. The amount you do not reinvest will, however, be subject to depreciation recapture and capital gain income tax liabilities. For

tax purposes, the amount you reinvest can be deferred. Pulling some of the proceeds from the next investment purchase is referred to as trading down in value.

When selling your relinquished property, you can carry an installment note. In what is commonly referred to as a carry back note, the note can either be included as part of your 1031 Exchange transaction or executed by you outside of the transaction. The transaction is a complex procedure and should always be reviewed with your legal and tax counsel before moving forward.

If you are looking for cash to put toward your next investment project or anything at all, you can complete the Forward 1031 Exchange process in a normal way, and when you buy your next property, buy it right. In other words, buy a property appraised for much higher than the sale price and refinance that property, pulling cash from the property in the refinance process. If you have good-paying tenants and you don't borrow so much that you are in a negative cash flow situation with that property, you have just secured cash not subject to capital gains taxes. Again, make sure you talk to your lender, accountant, and attorney before proceeding.

There are many other aspects to a 1031 Exchange to consider, such as business entity types in relationship the process, or trusts, and other forms of holdings and how an Exchange impacts them. However, I believe this is a very good place to wrap it up. If you take only one thing away from this chapter, let it be that if you are smart, and if you really want to become wealthy in real estate investing, you need to learn when and how to use a 1031 Exchange or employ someone who will do it for you. The 1031 Exchange is a completely legal way of deferring capital gains taxes, thus keeping more spendable dollars in your pocket. Many great books specific to 1031 Exchanges are available, and I recommend you buy one or two for your resource library.

# Chapter 9

## Conclusion, Other Tips, and Points of Interest
### Review Your Business Plan

A business plan is only as good as the person who executes it. If you write a business plan that projects a specific amount of income over a specific amount of time, your business plan also needs to drill down to a level that can be executed. For example, if you require 12 sales a year to meet your annual financial objectives that means you should have approximately 1 sale each month. We know, of course, that real estate doesn't really work like that and you might get two or three in one month and then not any for several months. Understanding, however, what your monthly budget requires to meet your objectives is critical to success.

Ask yourself what the requirements are for each week or drill down even further and ask yourself what is required each day to achieve that one-sale-a-month goal. As you begin to understand which methods of investing work best for you, you will begin to polish your skills to a point where you know exactly how many calls or contacts you must make to secure a solid opportunity. It isn't always perfect, but you should keep track of your calls and contacts at the beginning and when you secure a worthy investment opportunity count how many calls it took to achieve it. Do that the first two or three times. You will see that you likely have an average.

Let's say your average is one investment or sales opportunity every 15 calls or contacts. So, now you know that if you want to close 1 sale per month, you will need to make about 15 calls or contacts that month to achieve your goal. By taking the larger picture objectives and looking at your daily goal, you can both achieve the maximum and longer-term objective while making the process or method of achieving it very manageable.

Once we have completed a business plan and put your goals down on paper, they tend to become more real. Understanding how to break those goals into smaller sections so you can accomplish them makes the difference between being a success and being a failure. If your goals do seem very manageable to you in the daily "bite-size pieces," then you know that you have a plan that contains a foundation that can lead to success.

You do not want to set yourself up for failure. Establishing unrealistic goals in a business plan is a common mistake for a first time business owner of any type. If after you have broken your objectives into manageable activities and still find them difficult to attain, then perhaps your overall goals need revising.

This particular section of the book is about revisiting your business plan. As a small business owner and investor, you will always be learning something. You may find that 3 to 6 months from now the "strategy" you devised for your business is not the best way to approach future business. Trial and error, or as my grandfather used to say, "the school of hard knocks" is the best education you will ever receive. As you receive that education, the way you look at your business is going to change. It should change. Change in the business of investing is inevitable because the very market that we thrive on is changing every moment. As a result of either changes you want to make or changes that have come from other variables, your business plan will likely need changes.

The worst mistake you can make is to complete a business plan, put it in a one-half inch binder from the office supply store, file in on a shelf, and then never look at it again. You should be using the business plan as a system of checks and balances. To achieve success, you must be able to measure. And to measure, you must have something against which to measure. Your business plan should be a living checks and balances system for you. You will be grateful if you use it as the tool it can be and is intended to be.

If you ever need to seek capital funding or a bank loan in the future, your ability to measure yourself against your own objectives, and capable and flexible enough for making necessary changes on the fly, can go miles when it comes to a lender or capital investor making a financial support decision.

A living business plan is an example of your dedication to your company and your intelligence in relationship to good, old-fashioned business sense. Being able to alter your objectives on an as-needed basis to achieve greater rates of return and more dollars toward your bottom line is a business skill many believe can't be taught. I don't know about that . . . but I do know that it is something you need to teach yourself and something you will learn through dedication to the process.

Real estate investing, more so than other self-employed businesses, includes many areas for learning. In a bakery, you must understand baked goods. In a beauty salon, you must understand the latest trends, styles, and methods for creating them.

In real estate investing, the things you must learn are generally more expansive than the two previous examples. You need to learn the methods of locating your opportunities, negotiating the sale through either the seller or the bank, you need to learn about general home construction so that you can identify costly problems in a property on site, and then you need to learn about the art of preparing the home for sale to achieve a quick return on your investment. And you must learn the art of doing a financial analysis on each of your potential investment properties, and you need to learn the ins-and-outs of depreciation and taxation laws for your particular situation.

More is involved in investing in real estate than opening a beauty salon or a bakery, but there is also a great deal more reward if you learn the layers and make the commitment to never assume you have learned it all. In this business, everyday there is something to learn. Remember that the next time you pick up your business plan. Is it current? Does it contain the latest and greatest information to achieve long-term success for your company that you have in your head? If it's only in your head, and not in your plan, it may get lost when the next great piece of information, or idea, or education piles up on top of it.

Don't risk that chance. Look at it once a month and make sure it is right. If the plan is not right, then fix it. If you feel it is right, see if you can do anything to improve on it.

**Tax Benefits**

How tax savvy a businesswoman you are has a great effect on how much money is in your pocket at the end of the year. Tax codes allow you to deduct from your gross income costs for doing business. What you are left with is your net profit, otherwise referred to as net earnings. That amount is the amount that gets taxed, so the higher the number, the higher the taxes you pay. The lower that number, the lower the taxes. Obviously, deductions are paramount in keeping your dollars in your pockets.

As we have already established, knowing how to maximize your deductible business expenses lowers your taxable profit. When does the Internal Revenue Service (IRS) consider an expense a business tax-deductible expense?

## Ordinary and Necessary Expenses

Section 162 of the Internal Revenue Code is the cornerstone for determining the tax deductibility of every business expenditure. Here are the first several words:

Trade or business expenses. (a) In general. There shall be allowed as a deduction all the ordinary and necessary expenses paid or incurred during the taxable year in carrying on any trade or business . .

Section 162 goes on for what feels forever, but the important part is that expenses must be what is considered "ordinary and necessary" or they cannot be deducted. The tax code doesn't, however, define either what is ordinary or what is necessary. Luckily, in most cases, a legitimate business expense under section 162 is obvious, such as office supplies.

In some cases, such as travel, the IRS provides specific instructions for determining whether an expense is ordinary and necessary. This is often done through various IRS publications and regulations. It is entirely possible to get lost forever in the publications and regulations. Often one leads to another and so on. It's important to point out here that you will never entirely grasp all of the specific areas that apply to tax deductions. Some accountants and attorneys have invested their entire careers learning just that topic. If you don't understand a specific area, you are not alone—you are the majority, not the minority.

When a specific expense is not discussed in section 162 or in publications or regulations, federal courts have tried to figure out what Congress intended and apply it to a particular set of facts. The legal consensus is that ordinary and necessary refers to the purpose for which an expense is made. For example, having a cell phone plan is considered tax deductible for many businesses and their employees, but that is only accurate if those phones are being used to conduct business outside and away from normal office landlines. The courts have held that ordinary means "normal, common, and accepted under the circumstances by the business community." Necessary, on the other hand, is generally considered "appropriate and helpful."

Given those broad legal guidelines, it is not surprising that some folks have tried to push the envelope on ordinary and necessary business expenses. Be aware, however, that the IRS can push back at almost any time. Sometimes a compromise is reached, and sometimes the issue is thrown into a court's lap.

As ridiculous as it may sound, accountants and IRS professionals frequently rely on the "laugh test": Can you put down that business expense without laughing about putting one over on the IRS? If you can put it down and keep a straight face, then there may be some legitimacy to that expense. If you feel like you just got away with something by taking the deduction, you very likely may want to reconsider it because you won't actually know if you got away with it for quite some time.

**Large Expenses**
Because the IRS knows that people don't intentionally overpay for anything, amounts paid to them are usually not questioned. However, IRS auditors sometimes object to expenditures deemed unreasonably large under the circumstances.

While the tax code itself contains no "too big" limitation, courts have ruled that it should and can be considered. For example, it might be reasonable for a Realtor® to deduct a vehicle as a business expense.

However, it is unlikely that they will also be using a private jet for business, especially because their license is only good for the state in which they live and the jet schedule indicated that the majority of use was for trips to Jamaica.

**Personal Expenses**

The number one concern of the IRS is whether personal expenditures are being claimed as business expenses. For example, you cannot deduct the cost of commuting to work because the tax code specifically says this is a personal, not a business, expense. Fortunately, you can often arrange your affairs—legally—in a way that lets you derive considerable personal benefit and enjoyment from business expenditures.

It is legal to mix a little bit of pleasure with business. The trick is in the detail. Take the time to learn the basic details for each of those key areas so that you know your rights and limitations according to the law so you can maximize on the benefits while never crossing the legal line.

**Vehicle Expenses**

Operating a vehicle is expensive. The good news is that if you use your vehicle for business, or your business owns its own vehicle, you can deduct some of the costs of keeping it on the road. Mastering the rules of vehicle expense deductions can be tricky, but well worth your while.

There are two methods of claiming expenses: You can both keep track of and deduct all of your actual business related expenses, or you can deduct a certain amount for each mile plus all business-related tolls and parking fees.

As a rule, if you use a newer vehicle primarily for business, the actual expense method provides a larger deduction at tax time. If you use the actual expense method, you can also deduct depreciation on the vehicle. To qualify for the standard mileage rate, you must use it the first year you use a car for your business activity. You can't use the standard mileage rate if you have claimed accelerated depreciation deductions in prior years or have taken a section 179 deduction for the vehicle.

If your vehicle is used for both business and pleasure, only the business portion produces a tax deduction. That means you must keep track of how often you use the vehicle for business and total it at the end of the year. Certainly, if you own just one car or truck, no IRS auditor will let you get away with claiming that 100 percent of its use is related to your business.

## Start-Up Expenses for Your Business

The costs of getting a business started are capital expenses—$5,000 of which you may deduct the first year you're in business. Any remainder must be deducted in equal amounts over the next 15 years.

If you expect your business to make a profit immediately, you may be able to work around this rule by delaying paying some bills until after you're in business or by doing a small amount of business to officially start. But if, like many businesses, you will suffer losses during the first few years of operation, you might be better off taking the deduction over 5 years so you will have some profits to offset.

## Education Expenses

You can deduct education expenses if they are related to your current business, trade, or occupation. The expense must be to maintain or improve skills required in your present employment or be required by your employer or as a legal requirement of your job. The cost of education that qualifies you for a new job isn't deductible.

## Legal and Professional Fees

Fees that you pay lawyers, tax professionals, or consultants generally can be deducted in the year incurred. But if the work clearly relates to future years, they must be deducted over the life of the benefit you get from the lawyer or other professional.

Business books, including those that help you do without legal and tax professionals, are fully deductible as a cost of doing business.

## Bad Debts

If someone stiffs your business, the bad debt may or may not be deductible—it depends on the kind of product your business sells. See your accountant for more information.

If your business sells goods, you can deduct the cost of goods that you sell but aren't paid for. If, however, your business provides services, no deduction is allowed for time you devote to a client or customer who didn't pay. The rationale behind that rule is because it would be too easy for businesses to inflate bills and claim large deductions for bad debts.

## Business Entertaining

If you pick up the tab for entertaining present or prospective customers, you may deduct 50 percent of the cost if it is either:

• *directly related* to the business and business is discussed at the event—for example, a catered meeting at your office, or

• *associated with* the business, and the entertainment takes place immediately before or after a business discussion.

On the receipt or bill, always make a note of the specific business purpose -- for example, "Lunch with Joyce Slater of Ace Manufacturing Company to discuss widget contract."

## Travel

When you travel for business you can deduct many expenses including the cost of plane fare, costs of operating your vehicle, taxis, lodging, meals, shipping business materials, clothes cleaning, telephone calls, faxes, and tips. What about combining business and pleasure? It's okay, as long as business is the primary purpose of the trip. But if you take your family long, you can deduct only your own expenses, just as if you had traveled alone. The adjoining hotel room and the amusement park tickets might catch the auditor's eye.

## New Equipment

Some small businesses can write off the full cost of some assets in the year they buy them, rather than capitalizing them, in other words, deducting their cost over a number of years. Some assets don't qualify for a section 179 deduction, including real estate, inventory bought for resale, and property bought from a close relative.

## Interest

If you use credit to finance business purchases, the interest and carrying charges are fully tax deductible. The same is true if you take out a personal loan and use the proceeds for your business. Be sure to keep good records showing that the money was really put into your business. Otherwise, if you're audited later, the interest expense deduction could be disallowed because it's considered a personal expense.

## Moving Expenses

If you move because of your business or job, you may be able to deduct certain moving costs that would otherwise be nondeductible personal living expenses. To qualify, you must have moved in connection with your business. The new workplace must be at least 50 miles farther from your old home than your old workplace was.

## Software

As a general rule, software bought for business use must be depreciated over a 36-month period. But there are some important exceptions, so check with your accountant in regards to the specifics of software. However, don't forget about it come tax time.

## Charitable Contributions

Your business can make a charitable contribution and pass the deduction through to you to claim on your individual tax return if you have the appropriate incorporation. Determine what your business incorporation is and what the benefits of tax deductions are for you in this area.

If you've got some old computers or office furniture, giving it to a school or nonprofit organization can yield goodwill plus a tax benefit. But if the equipment has been fully depreciated (written off), you can't claim a deduction.

## Taxes

Taxes incurred in operating your business are generally deductible. How and when they are deducted depends on the type of tax.

• Sales tax on items you buy for your business's day-to-day operations is deductible as part of the cost of the items and not deducted separately. But tax on a big business asset, such as a vehicle, must be added to the vehicle's cost basis. Tax on the asset is not deductible entirely in the year the vehicle was bought.

• Excise and fuel taxes are separately deductible expenses.

• If your business pays employment taxes, the employer's share is deductible as a business expense. Self-employment tax is paid by individuals, not their businesses, and so isn't a business expense.

• Federal income tax paid on business income is never deductible. State income tax can be deducted on your federal return as an itemized deduction, not as a business expense.

• Real estate tax on property used for business is deductible, along with any special local assessments for repairs or maintenance. If the assessment is for an improvement—for example, to build a sidewalk—it isn't immediately deductible. Instead, it is deducted over a period of years.

## Advertising and Promotion

The cost of ordinary advertising of your goods or services, such as business cards or yellow page ads, is a deductible expense. Promotional costs that create business goodwill, for example, sponsoring a football team, are also deductible as long as there is a clear connection between the sponsorship and your business. For example, naming the team the "The Mini Investors" or listing the business name in the program is evidence of the promotion effort.

## Easily Overlooked Business Expenses

Here are some additional routine deductions that many business owners miss. Keep your eye out for them.

- audiotapes and videotapes related to business skills
- bank service charges
- business association dues
- business gifts
- business-related magazines and books
- casual labor and tips
- casualty and theft losses
- coffee and beverage service
- commissions
- consultant fees
- credit bureau fees
- office supplies
- online computer services related to business
- parking and meters
- petty cash funds
- postage
- promotion and publicity
- seminars and trade shows
- taxi and bus fare
- telephone calls away from the business

**Note:** Just because you didn't get a receipt does not mean you can't deduct the expense, so keep track of those small items and get big tax savings.

## Conclusion

It would take a lot more than 10 chapters to cover all there is to cover about real estate investing and that if you take that chance you will see infinite rewards. Making a real estate dollar is not the hardest dollar you will have made to this point in your life, and it is likely not ever going to be the hardest dollar you make going forward. Granted, you will have to stretch your wings and learn new things, but once you have mastered those areas you will be able to bring home the real estate investment dollar today.

Another great aspect of real estate investing is that there is no glass ceiling. In real estate investing, not only can you see the sky but you can do what it takes to reach it without anyone telling you that you can't and without bumping your head on the inevitable corporate glass ceiling that you didn't see coming.

Believe in yourself and that will take you farther than anything you learned in this book and anything you will learn about real estate investing going forward. Believe in yourself. I believe in you!

# Chapter #10

## Real Estate Dictionary

If you're a new real estate investor, the buying process can be a tricky one. New words, terms, and concepts are tossed around at an amazing pace. Often new investors fail to ask needed questions about the process and definition of terms. I know how it is. I was once a new investor. I wanted to appear sophisticated and "in the know," so many times I sat in silence and simply let learning opportunities pass me by.

To help the new real estate investor, I compiled some real estate terms with accompanying explanations or definitions. Here are some terms that you will most likely encounter as you purchase real estate. Familiarizing yourself with these home buying terms will help you make decisions regarding your purchase.

Keep these terms in mind as you go through the home buying process. Some title companies have books available free of charge that define many more terms. Spend some time learning all you can about real estate investing. That includes understanding terminology. If you don't understand something, be sure to ask.

# A

## Abstract
A succinct summary; (for example, an abstract of judgment; an abstract of title, an abstract plant.)

## Abstract of Judgment
Summary of a court judgment creating a lien against a property when filed with the county recorder.

## Abstract of Title
The condensed history of a title to a particular parcel of real estate, consisting of a summary of the original grant and all subsequent conveyances and encumbrances affecting the property and a certification by the abstractor that the history is complete and accurate.

## Abstract Plant
A collection of information and documents relating to title of a particular property. Also known as "title plant."

## Acceleration Clause
The clause in a mortgage or deed of trust that can be enforced to make the entire debt due immediately if the borrower defaults on an installment payment or other covenant.

## Acceptance
The written approval made by the seller from a buyer's offer.

## Accrued
On a closing statement, items of expense that are incurred but not yet payable, such as interest on a mortgage loan or taxes on real property.

## Addendum
Any addition or change to a contract.

Adjustable Rate Mortgage (ARM)
A loan with an interest rate that fluctuates based on a specified financial index, such as Treasury securities or the 11th District Cost of Funds.

Agent
A licensed representative of the state to conduct real estate transactions.

Agreement of Sale
Also known as an agreement to convey. A signed, written contract entered into between the seller (vendor) and buyer (vendee) for sale of real property (land) under certain specific terms and conditions.

Alienation
The transfer of property from one person to another. Alienation may be voluntary, such as by gift or sale, or involuntary, as through eminent domain or adverse possession.

Alienation Clause
A term of a mortgage requiring that the borrower pay in full the principal and interest due upon the sale of the property. (*See Acceleration or Due-on-Sale Clause*)

All-Inclusive Deed of Trust
A form of deed of trust that, in addition to any other amounts actually financed, includes the amounts of any prior deeds of trust. Sometimes referred to as a wrap-around or over-riding trust deed.

Amortization
Amortization is a schedule that outlines your loan payments for the duration of a loan. It details how much of each monthly payment goes toward the principal and how much goes toward paying off the loan balance. Initially, the bulk of your payments will be applied toward the interest. Many banks and title

companies offer free amortization books. Be sure to ask for your copy. They're a handy tool.

## Appraisal
Generally paid for by the buyer, the appraisal provides an estimate of a property's worth. Required by most lenders, it must be performed by a licensed appraiser before your home loan will be approved. The appraiser will arrive at a value based on the sale price of similar property. That is called "comparable" value.

## Appraise
To fix or set a price or value upon.

## Appreciation
The difference between the increased value of the property and the original value.

## Arrears
Generally, being overdue in an installment payment.

## Assessor
A municipality employee who estimates the value of properties for the purpose of taxes.

## Assignee
The person to whom a transfer of interest is made. Hence, an assignee of an Agreement of Purchase and Sale may buy the property and enforce the contract in the same fashion as the original party.

## Assignment
The method by which a right or contract is transferred from one person (the assignor) to another (the assignee).

## Assignor
The person who makes an assignment to another person.

Assumable Mortgage
A mortgage that can be taken over ("assumed") by the buyer when a home is sold. If interest rates have risen, an assumable mortgage at a low rate may prove a selling point for the property.

# B

Balloon Payment
A final payment of a mortgage loan that is considerably larger than the required periodic payments because the loan amount was not fully amortized.

Bankruptcy
An action filed in a federal bankruptcy court that allows a creditor to reorganize or discharge credit obligations due to insolvency. A property owner may halt foreclosure action by filing bankruptcy. Bankruptcies remain on a credit record for 7 years and can severely limit a person's ability to borrow.
• Chapter 7—"Debtor Wipeout." The court oversees the liquidation of the debtors' nonexempt assets, distributing the cash proceeds proportionally among creditors.
• Chapter 11—A Chapter 11 is a business reorganization proceeding.
• Chapter 13—"Debtor Workout." A Workout is the almost-automatic choice of most trustors seeking to use a bankruptcy filing to delay the inevitable trustee's sale as long as they can. The purpose of this proceeding is to give a wage earner time for rehabilitation . . . a temporary respite free from the collection efforts of creditors.

Beneficiary
A person entitled to receive money or assets from a trust or an estate. A lender is a beneficiary with a deed of trust or a note as a security for a loan.

**Betterment**
Any improvement of real estate that results in a rise in market value of that property.

**Bid**
An offer by an intending purchaser to pay a designated price for property that is about to be sold at auction.

**Bill of Sale**
Written document by which title to personal property (goods or chattels) is transferred from one party to another.

**Blanket Deed of Trust**
A deed of trust secured by more than one lot or parcel of land.

**Borrower**
The individual to whom a thing or money is lent at his request.

**BPO**
Brokers Price Opinion.

**Breach**
The breaking or violating of a law, a right, obligation, engagement, or duty, either by commission or omission.

**Broker**
An agent authorized by the state to deal in real estate.

**Brokerage**
The bringing together of two or more parties interested in making a real estate transaction.

**Buy-Down mortgage**
A financing technique used to reduce the monthly payments for the first few years of a loan. Funds in the form of discount points are given to the lender by the builder or seller to buy down or

lower the effective interest rate paid by the buyer, thus reducing the monthly payments for a set time.

Buyer's Broker (*Buyer's Agent, Buyer's Representative*)
A Buyer Broker, as opposed to a Listing Broker, represents only the interests of the buyer. For a broker (also referred to as agent sometimes) to be considered a buyer's broker, an agreement must be made between the buyer and the broker. Without such an agreement, the agent could end up representing the seller in a real estate transaction. In most states we now have what's call "Limited Dual Agency." Under this theory, a broker can represent both the buyer and the seller. I, for one, don't see how this is good for either the buyer or seller. If you as a buyer want to use a Broker, get a Buyer Broker Agreement signed. You can download one free of charge at www.oaprei.com/Buyer%20Broker%20Agreement.pdf As Martha Stewart says, "It's a good thing."

Buyers Market
A market condition where there are fewer buyers than there are sellers. Usually indicated when a property is on the market for more than 90 days and interest rates are very high. (12 percent or higher)

# C

Capital Gain
A profit earned from the sale of an asset.

Cash Flow
The surplus after paying operating expenses and mortgage payments.

Certificate of Sale
A certificate issued at a judicial sale entitling the buyer to receive a deed after confirmation of court for the purchase of the property.

Chain of Title
A succession of conveyances comprising the title record history to a specific parcel of real property.

Chattel
Personal property, such as household items.

Chattel Mortgage
A mortgage secured by personal property.
Closing Costs
This is the final step in the home buying/selling process. The loan documents are signed and finalized at this point. After the documents are signed, notarized, and the money submitted to satisfy all the debts, the transfer of the deed is made from the buyer to the seller when the title company (or attorney) files the deed and any supporting documentation with the country clerk. The filing of the documents with the county clerk signifies closing has occurred.

Closing Date
The agreed-upon date for a buyer to take over property.

Cloud on Title
Any outstanding claim that contradicts the title record, and if valid, would impair the owner's title.

Code
A collection of laws relating to a certain topic, such as real property or patents.

Cosigner
A cosigner signs a promissory note and takes responsibility for the debt.

Collateral
Real estate or personal property pledged as security for a debt.

Collection
Obtaining payment or the liquidation of a debt or claim, either by personal solicitation or legal proceedings.

Comparables
Similar properties used as yardsticks to determine the market value of a certain property.

Complaint
The original or initial pleading by which an action is commenced; a written statement of the essential facts constituting the offense charged.

Condemnation
A judicial or administrative proceeding to exercise the power of eminent domain, through which a government agency takes private property for public use and compensates the owner.

Contingency
A specified condition that must be fulfilled before a contract becomes firm and binding.

Contract
An agreement between two or more persons creating an obligation to do or not to do a particular thing.

Conventional Loan
A loan that requires no insurance or guarantees.

Conveyance
A written instrument that transfers title to or an interest in land from one party to another (for example, a deed, an assignment, or a bill of sale)

Counteroffer
A response given to an offer.

Credit report
A document from a credit bureau setting forth a credit rating and pertinent financial data concerning a person or a company and used by banks, merchants, suppliers and the like in evaluating a credit risk.

Creditor
One to whom money is owed.

**D**

Debt
A sum of money due by a certain and express agreement; a specified sum of money owing to one person from another, including not only obligation of debtor to pay but the right of the creditor to receive and enforce payment.

Debt Ratio
To compare the total monthly payments of all of the borrower's debts (including the mortgage) with the gross monthly income of the borrower. It evaluates the borrower's ability to pay mortgage. Also referred to as Debt-to-Income ratio.

Debtor
An entity that owes a debt; one who owes a debt.

Decree of Foreclosure
A court order to set out the outstanding amount on a delinquent mortgage in order to sell the property to pay the mortgagee.

Deed
A written instrument that, when executed and delivered, conveys title to or an interest in real estate.

## Deed in Lieu of Foreclosure

A process whereby the owner, with the approval of the lender, deeds the property to the lender to avoid foreclosure. Lenders are generally reluctant to accept a deed in lieu unless the title is free and clear of any other encumbrances junior to theirs and the owners execute an estoppel affidavit acknowledging that they are acting volitionally, with informed consent.

## Deed of Reconveyance

An instrument that releases and discharges a deed of trust, when the mortgage has been paid out.

## Deed of Trust (Trust Deed)

A three party security instrument conveying the legal title to real property as security for the repayment of a loan. The owner is called the trustor. The neutral third party to whom the bare legal title is conveyed (and who is called on to liquidate the property if need be) is the trustee. The lender is the beneficiary. When the loan is paid off, the trustee is directed by the beneficiary to issue a deed of reconveyance to the trustor, which extinguishes the trust deed lien.

## Default

The failure to make payments in full on time or at all or to live up to any other obligations placed on the borrower by the loan agreement.

## Defeasance Clause

A clause used in leases and mortgages that cancels a specified right upon the occurrence of a certain condition, such as cancellation of a mortgage upon repayment of the mortgage loan.

## Defendant

The person who defends against a claim asserted in a court action.

Deficiency Judgment
A judgment entered in a lawsuit when a property is sold for less than the amount of the loan.

Delinquency
A condition when the payment is late but not yet in default.

Demand Letter
Also known as a Breach Letter or Notice of Intent to Foreclose. Notice to the borrower that he/she is in "breach" of the terms of the Note and advising of the right to cure the default. Department of Housing and Urban Development (HUD) A federal agency focusing on programs regarding housing and renewal of city communities.

Department of Veterans Affairs (VA)
An independent federal agency overseeing programs for military veterans, including loan and mortgage programs. This agency allows most veterans to purchase a house without a down payment.

Disclosure Statement
Document disclosing the terms of a loan.

Due-on-Sale Clause
A clause in a mortgage that requires that the mortgage be paid out in full upon the sale of the property.

Due Diligence
Such a measure of prudence, activity, or assiduity as is properly to be expected from a reasonable and prudent man under the particular circumstance.

# E

Earnest Money Deposit
Along with an offer, buyers can make a deposit on the home to demonstrate the seriousness of the offer. When an earnest money deposit is made, it is held by an escrow until closing. It is then added to the down payment.

Easement
A right of way allowing someone to cross over another's property for certain purposes, such as power lines or water mains.

Encroachment
A fixture that illegally intrudes into or invades the property or encloses a portion of it, diminishing its width or area.

Encumbrance
Anything, such as a mortgage, tax, or judgment lien, an easement, or restriction on the use of the land or an outstanding dower right that may diminish the value or use and enjoyment of a property.

Equity
The surplus of value that may remain after existing liens are deducted from the property.

Equity Right of Redemption
The right to avoid foreclosure action by paying off the debts, interest, and fees that accumulated on the property.

Escrow Account
Funds held before closing by a third party, usually including the earnest money deposit. Future taxes and homeowners insurance, held by the mortgage company after closing, are also considered escrow.

**Estate**
The total assets a person has when he dies, including real property.

**Estoppel Certificate**
A certificate in which a borrower certifies the amount owed on a mortgage loan and the rate of interest.

**Eviction**
The act of depriving a person of the possession of land or rental property held or leased.

**F**

**Fair Market Value**
The amount at which property would change hands between a willing buyer and a willing seller, neither being under any compulsion to buy or sell and both having reasonable knowledge of the relevant facts.

**Fannie Mae**
It's an official name of the Federal National Mortgage Association, which is one of the largest agencies that buys mortgages from lenders and resells them as securities on the secondary mortgage market.

**FHA – Federal Housing Administration**
FHA is a branch of the Department of Housing and Urban Development (HUD). The agency's basic function is to direct housing in a way that Congress mandates by issuing mortgage insurance to institutional lenders on the loans they make. With such loan insurance, lenders are willing to lend with smaller down payments and at lower rates of interest.

**FHA Loans**
A loan program offering low-rate mortgages to buyers willing to make a down payment as little as 3 percent.

First Mortgage
A mortgage that is in first position and has priority as a lien over all other mortgages.

FSBO – For Sale By Owner
This term refers to property being sold without a real estate broker. FSBO is also used to refer to the homeowner who is selling the property.

Foreclosure
A legal procedure whereby property used as security for a debt is sold to satisfy the debt in the event of default in payment of the mortgage note or default of other terms in the mortgage document. The foreclosure procedure brings the rights of all parties to a conclusion and passes the title in the mortgaged property to either the holder of the mortgage or a third party who may purchase the realty at the foreclosure sale, free of all encumbrances affecting the property subsequent to the mortgage.

# G

Garnishment
A statutory proceeding whereby a person's property, money, credits in possession or under the control of, or owing by, another are applied to payment of the former's debt to third person by proper statutory process against debtor and garnishee.

Good Faith Estimate
Institutional lender estimates the costs a borrower will incur, including inspection fees and loan processing charges.

Grace Period
A period of days during which a debtor may cure a delinquency without penalty (before triggering a late charge, a foreclosure, or an acceleration of the balance due).

Grantee
The person to whom the title of the property is granted.

Grantor
The person (seller) who grants title to another person (buyer).

# H

Habendum Clause
Meaning "to have and to hold," which defines the quantity of the estate transferred to the new owner of land.

Home Equity Line of Credit
Sometimes referred to as an HELOC, a Home Equity Line of Credit is a loan that a property owner secures that can be repaid and borrowed again at the owner's convenience.

Home Equity Loan
Borrowing against the equity in one's home.

HUD 1 Statement
A form, usually given by a bank, that includes the costs of purchasing a home.

Hypothecate
When you use something as security and still retain possession of it.

# I

Indemnify
Any losses and damages an individual endures for which you are fully responsible.

Instrument
A legal written document.

Involuntary lien
A lien issued against a property without an owner's approval.

# J

Joint Ownership
When two or more parties own the same property.

Joint Venture
A project where two or more individuals take part in a business transaction to share the cost, risk, and reward.

Judgment
The final decision of the court resolving a dispute and determining the rights and obligations of the parties.

Judicial Foreclosure
A foreclosure process executed through a court action.

Junior lien
A lien that is subordinate or junior to a senior lien.

# L

Land Contract
An agreement used to sell real property that transfers ownership of the property, but the title does not transfer until most or the entire purchase price is paid.

Landlord
He who, being the owner of an estate of land, or rental property, leased it to another.

Lease
An agreement involving payment of rent for possession of real estate for a specific period of time.

**Lease Option**
A lease that contains the right to purchase a property for a specific price during a given time frame.

**Lender**
He from whom a thing or money is borrowed.

**Lien**
A claim or charge on a property for payment of some debt, obligation or duty.

**Life Estate**
An estate whose duration is limited to the life of the party holding it.

*Lis pendens*
A term meaning "legal action pending," giving notice of an action or proceeding affecting the title of the property.

**Loss Mitigation Department**
A department that helps homeowners avoid foreclosure; the lender tries to help a borrower who has been unable to make loan payments and in danger of defaulting on a loan

**Lot Book Report**
A title record report given by a title company announcing encumbrances recorded against the property.

# M

**Marketable Title**
A title with no claims or defects that could otherwise hinder a property being sold.

**Mechanic's lien**
A claim created by state statutes for the purpose of securing priority of payment of the price or value of work performed and

materials furnished in erecting or repairing a building or other structure, and as such, attaches to the land as well as buildings and improvements erected thereon.

Mortgage
An interest in land created by a written instrument providing security for the performance of a duty or the payment of a debt.

Mortgagee
The entity, usually a bank or financial institution that lends money to a borrower.

Mortgagor
The person borrowing money from a lender to purchase a property.

Multiple Listings Service (MLS) A listing of properties from local real estate agents that consist of homes available in an area. For-Sale-by-owner properties are not listed in this database.

**N**

NARCA
National Association of Retail Collection Attorneys

Notice of Default (NOD)
A notice sent by a lender when a mortgage payment is late in an attempt to cure or make the loan current.

Notice of Rescission
A legal document used when the defaulting party either cured or corrected a default.

Notice of Sale
The notice of an impending foreclosure sale the state requires. The notice recites the legal description of the property being

foreclosed upon and gives the time, date, and place of the pending sale.

# O

Offer to Purchase
A contract expressing a person's willingness to purchase a certain property on terms expressed in the offer.

Owner Financing (Seller Financing) A creative method in real estate where the seller of a property agrees to finance all or some of the property. In a sense, the owner acts as a bank.

# P

Power of Attorney
A written document signed by the owner that authorizes someone else to act in behalf of the owner.

Power of Sale
A clause commonly inserted in mortgages and deeds of trust that are in default, giving the mortgagee (or trustee) the right and power to advertise and sell the mortgaged property at public auction to satisfy the debt.

Pre-Foreclosure
Term used to discuss delinquent properties before they go to the foreclosure auction.

# Q

Quit Title
An action to remove an adverse claim or cloud from the title of property.

Quit Claim Deed
A deed of conveyance that releases any title, interest, or claim the grantor may have in the premises.

# R

Real Estate Owned (REO)
Property acquired by the lender after it went to auction.

Recorder
A public official responsible for keeping the records of real estate transactions.

Redemption Period
The time allotted to the mortgagor to reclaim property after being sold at an auction. Not all states have a redemption period.

# S

Sales Contract
A contract to which the buyer and seller agree to terms of sale.

Second Mortgage
A second loan placed upon a property in addition to an existing first loan.

Seller Financing
A creative method in real estate where the seller of a property agrees to finance all or some of the property. In a sense, the owner acts like a bank.

Sellers Market
When the market conditions are such that the sellers have the advantage and multiple offers are made.

Sheriff's Sale
The sale of a property to satisfy a debt or judgment.

Short Sale
The sale of a property under or at market value lower than the loan balance.

Simultaneous Closing
The term "simultaneous closing" refers to two closings occurring at the same time. This is a creative technique used when traditional financing will not work.

Subject To
The transfer of rights to pay a debt from one party to another, with the original party remaining liable for the debt if the second party defaults.

Survey
The process by which a parcel of land is measured and its boundaries and contents set forth.

## T

Tax Deed
A type of deed used to convey title after real property is sold at auction by public authority for nonpayment of taxes.

Tax Lien
A lien on real estate in favor of a state or local government that may be foreclosed on for the nonpayment of taxes.

Tenant
A person in possession of real property with the owner's permission.

Tenant at Sufferance
A person who after rightfully being in possession of a rented premises continues to live in that premises after his right has terminated.

Tenant at Will
One who holds possession of premises with the owner's permission.

Title
Evidence of ownership of land.

Title Company
Firms that examine properties to ensure that the title to a piece of property is clear and free of any encumbrances. They also issue title insurance.

Title Insurance
An insurance policy that provides protection for lenders and buyers against any losses caused by defects in the title.

Title Report
A report which sets out the current state of title to a property.

Title Search
A search within the public records to determine ownership and that there are no claims or liens against the property.

Torrens Title
A Torrens Title contains a listing of all legal instruments (mortgages, judgments, liens) that have been recorded on the property from its origin.

Trust Account
A special account used by a broker or escrow agent to safeguard funds for a buyer or seller.

Trust Deed
A three party security instrument conveying the legal title to real property as security for the repayment of a loan. The owner is called the trustor. The neutral third party to whom the bare legal

title is conveyed (and who is called on to liquidate the property if need be) is the trustee. The lender is the beneficiary. When the loan is paid off, the trustee is directed by the beneficiary to issue a deed of reconveyance to the trustor, which extinguishes the trust deed lien.

Trustee
A legally empowered person who holds or controls a piece of property for another person.

Trustee's Deed
A deed given to the successful high bidder after a foreclosure auction.

Trustee's Sale
An auction where a trustee may sell a property that has defaulted in effort to pay the outstanding debt that is owed.

**U**

UCC
Uniform Commercial Code; uniform laws drafted by the National Conference of Commissioners on Uniform State Laws governing commercial transactions.

Undivided Interest
Ownership of real estate by joint tenants under the same title.

Unsecured Debt
Debt not secured by collateral.

Upset Price
The opening bid amount that begins the auction bidding during a foreclosure sale.

# V

### VA Loans
A program that allows the purchase of a house without a down payment to most veterans.

### Vacate
To make vacant or empty.

# W

### Warranty Deed
Deed in which the grantor warrants good clear title.

### Without Recourse
Giving the lender no right to seek payment or seize assets in the event of nonpayment from anyone other than the party specified in the debt contract.

### Wraparound Mortgage
The financing technique in which payment of the existing mortgage is continued by the seller and a new, higher interest loan (larger than the existing mortgage) is paid by the borrower.

# Y

### Yield
The return on investment or the amount of profit stated as a percentage of the amount invested.

# Z

### Zoning
Regulations that control the use of land within a jurisdiction.

www.ingramcontent.com/pod-product-compliance
Lightning Source LLC
Chambersburg PA
CBHW051518170526
45165CB00002B/519